Praise for *The Father's House*

"If you want to know the meaning of life, if you long to know who you are and Whose you are, if your heart aches to love and to be loved, this book will guide you to the answers and bring you into communion with the One who holds them."

— From the Foreword by Sister Bethany Madonna, SV

"Elegantly written, *The Father's House* explores the human experience in light of Trinitarian theology to delve into the true meaning of our existence. It is both accessible to the average reader and packed with the profound truths of the Faith."

— Edward Sri, theologian and author of *The Art of Living*

"This book is a profound retreat for the mind and heart. It is a clear, luminous, and concentrated meditation on the mystery of Christianity for our practical and spiritual lives. Father Brent seeks to interpret the inner life of the human soul from the perspective of eternity, seeing the created order in light of the Trinity, and understanding the human person as a spiritual creature made for the Trinity. This is a book that invites and challenges us to a greater interiority and a closer proximity to the mystery of Christ."

— Thomas Joseph White, OP,
Rector, Angelicum, Rome

"In this highly accessible text, Father James draws on the essence of the Gospel and the universal ascetical-mystical tradition of Christianity to articulate a lucid and prayerful introduction to the great principles of the spiritual life. Many Catholics are unaware of the lofty vocation that is ours as baptized Christians. This book presents a highly accessible synthetic articulation of the Christian vocation to 'become and to be Christ.'"

— Matthew K. Minerd, Ph.D., Professor of Philosophy
and Moral Theology, Byzantine Catholic Seminary,
Pittsburgh, PA and Program Director, MA in Philosophy,
Holy Apostles College and Seminary, Cromwell, CT

"With engaging clarity, from the heights of the Trinity to the depths of the heart, this son of Saint Dominic opens wide the doors to the Father's House. Speaking the language of Sacred Scripture, Father Brent assembles the wisdom of the saints—including Elizabeth of the Trinity, Thérèse of Lisieux, Mother Teresa, and John Paul II, as well as Rublev and other important voices in Eastern Christianity—to baptize our minds in the *communio* of the Church and make the case for a life of personal conversion, contemplation, and holy friendship."

— Professor Anthony Lilles, St. Patrick's Seminary and University

"Father James Brent is in awe of the Trinity! He gives a beautiful witness to behold—an invitation for you, too. You are not meant to be separated from the Father, Son, and Holy Spirit. You are meant to live in the heart of the Trinity, in merciful love and eternal victory. Don't delay. Let the Trinity guide you to the fullness of the Christian life through the words of this humble and wise friar."

— Kathryn Jean Lopez, senior fellow, National Review Institute and author of *A Year with the Mystics: Visionary Wisdom for Daily Living*

"'We have inherited a universal pathological condition or affliction of the heart,' observes Dominican Father James Brent in his inspiring book *The Father's House*. It is a condition that leaves us feeling spiritually homeless. The answer to it is the Father's House—an invitation from Jesus Christ that promises: "*I have everything you could ever need or want. I am opening it all up to you now and bringing you into it. I am making a place for you. All of it is yours. My whole life with the Father is yours."* This is a book of extraordinary insight and encouragement by a much-revered teacher, preacher, and spiritual master."

— Father Peter John Cameron, OP,
Editorial Director, Aleteia.org | English edition

THE FATHER'S HOUSE

THE FATHER'S HOUSE

DISCOVERING OUR HOME
IN THE TRINITY

By James Dominic Brent, OP

Foreword by Sister Bethany Madonna, SV

BOOKS & MEDIA

Boston

Nihil Obstat: Reverend Basil Cole, O.P.

Imprimi Potest: Very Reverend Allen B. Moran, O.P.
        Prior Provincial of the Dominican Province of Saint Joseph
        April 20, 2023

Library of Congress Control Number: 2023935889
CIP data is available.

ISBN 10: 0-8198-2759-2
ISBN 13: 978-0-8198-2759-3

Published by Pauline Books & Media, 50 Saint Paul's Avenue, Boston, MA 02130-3491

Printed in the U.S.A.

www.pauline.org

Pauline Books & Media is the publishing house of the Daughters of St. Paul, an international congregation of women religious serving the Church with the communications media.

1 2 3 4 5 6 7 8 9   28 27 26 25 24 23

To Saint Joseph

Contents

Foreword

I<small>T WAS THE</small> summer before my final vows and I was beginning a thirty-day retreat in anticipation. I had prepared a seemingly impressive day-by-day plan for my meditations, and I felt pretty good going in. All of that changed in an instant, on day one, as I listened to the first reading at Mass. It was the story of Jacob, who disguised himself as his older brother Esau to dupe their father, Isaac, into giving him the blessing of the firstborn instead (see Gen 27:1–29). I had never been struck by this passage before, but it was as if a ray of light pierced me to the core. I had the inexplicable conviction that *I* do this. That I feel a need to "dress up" so that God the Father will bless me, to try to impress him or make him think I am someone better than I am, somehow deserving of his blessing. Slowly, I began to realize I had been operating out of misconceptions of God, or shame over my own sinfulness and weakness, or fear of being rejected and punished. It was a clear invitation to come close, to come to know the Father and to receive his blessing as I am, purely and without any pretenses.

"The Father himself loves you" (Jn 16:27). As if for the first time, the truth of this reality penetrated my heart and freed me to receive and live from my identity as a beloved daughter of the Father, made one with Christ Jesus, and anointed with the Holy Spirit and power.

As I read *The Father's House: Discovering Our Home in the Trinity*, this transformative grace was renewed. Father James Brent delves into what seems to be a best-kept secret.

Jesus said to the Samaritan woman, "If you knew the gift of God . . ." (Jn 4:10), referring to himself, the living water she was thirsting for. If only we knew this gift of God . . . our joy would be complete! (See Jn 15:11.)

Father James masterfully, with clarity and simplicity, draws us into the gift of God—who has revealed himself as the Blessed Trinity, Father, Son, and Holy Spirit, a life-giving communion of love. By giving us a practical, human, and scriptural exposition of how to live this truth that sets us free to live in love and taste the promised abundance, this book also offers us joy as a natural consequence.

We can, however, be prevented from living the full expression of this gift if we are unaware of our fallen nature or how to cooperate in the grace available to us in Christ. As if shining light into darkness, *The Father's House* illumines the "pathos of the heart," and we come to understand the wound original sin left on our experience of ourselves, others, and the world. We come to understand how we can be influenced by the enemy with a myriad of temptations, unruly passions, distractions, and disordered affections. Outlining practical means, Father James encourages us to recognize and resist these movements by engaging in the sacramental life and employing the undaunted authority of our Baptism.

In Baptism, our Father's love goes to the furthest extremes: indwelling. Jesus said, "Those who love me will keep my word, and my Father will love them, and we will come to them and make our home with them" (Jn 14:23). We become one with Jesus in Baptism. And as Father James impresses upon us, it is in this sacrament that "you become Jesus." The Trinity comes to dwell in our souls.

As you read on, it becomes evident that God asks us for more, calling us to live out a Christian life of service, because he can provide us with more. He has poured the Holy Spirit into our hearts. Living the Beatitudes opens us to a life of friendship in union with God. We realize that our blessedness does not come from our wealth or surplus, but rather from our happy poverty and vulnerable dependence on the Trinity.

If you want to know the meaning of life, if you long to know who you are and Whose you are, if your heart aches to love and to be loved, this book will guide you to the answers and bring you into communion with the One who holds them.

SISTER BETHANY MADONNA, SV
+ *Holy Thursday, April 6, 2023*

Acknowledgments

THE PRESENT BOOK never would have come to be without the contribution and support of many people along the way. The numerous Catholic campus ministries and young adult groups across the country who invited me to speak or lead their retreats have my special gratitude. Everything in this book is a response to their questions, their hunger for God, and their desire to follow Christ. Particular thanks go to the Fellowship of Catholic University Students (FOCUS) for so many invitations to lead weekend retreats and to serve as chaplain for their Summer Projects program time and again. It is some of the students of Summer Projects whose story I tell in Chapter Five, and I shall never forget the grace of so many summer days and nights in the Rockies. Special gratitude to the college chaplains along the way who encouraged me to write this book.

Years back, Father Benedict Croell, OP, and I traveled the country together for one year of full-time preaching on campuses. He was the organizational genius behind the whole campaign and an inspirational example of zeal for souls and fidelity to Dominican life on the road. I shall be forever grateful to him for the adventure and for keeping everything properly paced. Our cloistered Dominican Nuns and active Dominican Sisters also deserve abundant thanks. It was their prayers and sacrifices that obtained whatever fruits have come from our preaching. Many thanks to Father Bruno Shah, OP, who patiently read an early draft of this book and offered very valuable comments. I'm equally grateful to Sister Diana Marie, OP, of the Hawthorne Dominican Sisters, who also read an early manuscript, made valuable comments, and clarified the details of the story of Rose Hawthorne in Chapter Six. Truly, this book is a fruit of the whole Dominican family.

The Daughters of Saint Paul played a large role in bringing everything to completion and I am very grateful. Sister Marie Paul, FSP, believed in the project from the beginning, watched over its growth with care, and has been most encouraging through the entire process. Courtney Saponaro graciously offered many helpful suggestions and greatly improved the work overall and Matthew Igoe was of special editorial assistance. Many others served in this book's production and the whole team at Pauline Books and Media has my deepest appreciation. Special thanks also to Sister Bethany Madonna, SV, for graciously writing the Foreword.

"Not to us, O LORD, not to us, but to thy name give glory" (Ps 115:1).

Introduction

EVERY HUMAN BEING carries, in the depths of his or her heart, three fundamental questions. First, the purpose question: *What is the purpose of life?* Second, the identity question: *Who am I?* Third, the love question: *How do I find love?* You and I cannot really live or flourish without solid and true answers to the three questions, and how we answer them is decisive for the direction of our lives. The aim of this book is to offer answers, not according to one more theory or worldview currently on offer in our culture's marketplace of ideas, but according to the Gospel of Jesus Christ as the Church has lived it and understood it for thousands of years. The Gospel is essentially the announcement that God himself has opened up the way for us to go to him—to live in the Father's House in the heavenly places. It is the way of friendship with Jesus Christ, drinking deeply of his Spirit of Love, in the great *communio* of the Church.

The first three chapters of the book lay out the Gospel answers to the three questions. Once we have learned these answers, the next question becomes how to live according to what we've learned—how to walk in the way of friendship with the eternal Son of God in our midst. The second three chapters, therefore, lay out some traditional, time-tested, and true guidance on the practicals of the way. The way of friendship with Jesus Christ is essentially a path to radical healing of the heart, a supernatural healing and elevation of our souls, a renewal of the image of God in us by grace. Chapter Four starts down the path of healing by telling of a certain illness or pathos of the heart coming down to us from the fall—a primordial event of sin at the origins of the human race that affects us all. Learning something of the effects of the fall reveals much about ourselves, our conditions, and our identities. Next, Chapter Five unpacks the law of love by which we are called to live, and Chapter Six explores the Beatitudes, since the law of love and the Beatitudes sum up the whole way of friendship. Like life itself, the whole book leads in the end to the Father's House.

For God has been pleased to adopt us in Jesus Christ, and this book is essentially an extended meditation on the meaning of filial adoption by grace—what it is and how to live it. The expression *filial adoption* might sound abstract and removed from real life, but the mystery it names is most real and concrete. This book is not academic, but was born from real life. It was born from years of offering retreats, campus missions, a variety of talks, and spiritual direction to college students and young adults all over the United States and beyond. It was born from thousands of conversations and ministry events with young people over more than a decade— including many people who have suffered much in their lives.

Real people raised their real questions and found real answers in the grace and truth of filial adoption. Those personal conversations and pastoral circumstances have inspired the writing style of this book. For the aim of the book is *communio*: "so that you may have fellowship with us" (1 Jn 1:3).

In the great *communio* of the holy Church of God, ancient curses are broken, old sins are washed away, and the demons of days gone by are finally put to flight. Something new begins in the soul by grace. What begins is eternal life—personal familiarity with the living God who dwells in unapproachable Light (see 1 Tim 6:16). Thanks to our Baptism, he shines now in the depths of our hearts to give us a knowledge of his glory shining on the face of Jesus Christ (see 2 Cor 4:6). What has begun at the center of our souls is a new perception of the Presence, an awareness of divine Love, a true taste of first fruits from the new world to come. It tastes like "joy based on the truth."[1]

---

1. Saint Augustine, *Confessions*, trans. Henry Chadwick (Oxford: Oxford University Press, 1992), X.xxiii.33, 199.

CHAPTER ONE

The Holy Trinity

WHAT IS THE purpose of life? There could hardly be a more fundamental question, and how one answers this question establishes the orientation of one's entire life. Many people, it seems, live for some package of personally preferred earthly goods: pleasure, money, power, honor, success, relationships, social and political causes, or some combination of such things. Such things are good in themselves, but in the end no package of earthly goods can perfectly or ultimately satisfy us. For in the end, the purpose of our lives is either God or something other than God, and everything other than God is far *less* than God. Anything less than God is something finite. And nothing finite satisfies the human heart—not perfectly, not ultimately. Yet in what sense could *God* be the purpose of life? How could God ever be the joy of our hearts? The answer comes to us in the Gospel of Jesus Christ. The Gospel is called good news precisely because it is the explanation of how God has become the purpose and the joy of our hearts by grace.

All human beings are able to know at least *something* of the existence of God and his attributes just by reflecting upon the world of nature. Although we cannot sense God directly like things in the environment, God is also not simply hidden from us. For the whole world of nature is essentially an order of signs from God—especially the greatness and beauty of the world (see Wis 13:1–9; Ps 19; Sir 42:15–43:33; Rom 1:19–20). What is going on within God, however—his interior life and ultimate purpose for creating the world—is simply an unknown to human reason. Looking at the world of nature will not tell us. It is his secret to share, and in the Gospel, he shares it.

Everyone has an inner life. It conceals who we really are in some sense and our reasons for doing what we do. What is going on inside us, and our true intentions, are not always revealed to those on the outside. God too has such an inner life. Yet the story comes down to us from the prophets and apostles of old that God has revealed his inner life to them. It began with a gradual revelation of his secret *plan* for the world, and it led up to the revelation of a secret *personal life* he enjoys within himself. The secret of his interior personal life is called the mystery of the Holy Trinity. The mystery of the Trinity is that the one God is Father, Son, and Holy Spirit—three divine persons in one divine essence. Such a revelation of the inner life of God is mysterious indeed, but it is not meaningless. On the contrary, the Trinity is most meaningful thing of all. How so?

Every day, Catholics make the sign of the Cross and say: "In the name of the Father, and of the Son, and of the Holy Spirit." Few Catholics fully realize, however, the mystery and the magnitude of the words. The words tell us the reason for the world. God created it all—the sun, moon, and stars, the seas, all they contain, the dry land too, and all of humanity—so that we might enter into the amazing and awe-inspiring life of the Father, Son, and Holy Spirit. The purpose of life, then, is for us to enter into the Holy Trinity.

A First Encounter with the Holy Trinity

The Holy Trinity created us in order to adopt us. The great work of God, the God who is three in one, is to take us into his House and make us his own in love. The point is simply for us to live in God, and enjoy God, forever. For what could be better than God? What could be better than knowing, loving, and enjoying the Holy Trinity? Such a proposal might sound abstract, or rather removed from our experience, but in fact it touches on real life. I have seen it speak to the deepest questions of the human heart.

Many years ago, when I was a deacon, a young woman approached me, making inquiries about the Catholic Church. She was raised a Mormon but had ceased practicing during high school. She looked into evangelical Christianity, but she was still searching for something more. She had a Catholic boyfriend at the time and wanted to learn something about the Catholic faith to impress him, but she insisted explicitly that she would never become Catholic. In

our first meeting, she asked about the main teaching of the
Catholic Church. I replied that the primary teaching and the
main point of God's revelation to us is the mystery of the
Holy Trinity. As the conversation continued, she found the
Holy Trinity deeply captivating. Indeed, it struck her so
much that she began to investigate the Catholic Church
more seriously, and contrary to her initial declaration, she
eventually entered the catechumenate.

Over the course of months, her pondering of the Trinity
continued and her captivation grew. When the time came to
discuss the mystery of the Trinity in her weekly catechetical
sessions, her anticipation was real and her excitement was
great. By this point, she had developed many relationships
with Catholics, and she told them how excited she was to discuss the Holy Trinity. Much to her dismay, the typical response
from her Catholic friends was something like this: "Oh, the
Trinity? Well, don't worry about it. It's just a mystery."

As sometimes happens, the convert understood the significance of the Trinity more than the cradle Catholics. For
her, the Holy Trinity was the key that opened the door to a
new and higher form of life, greater than anything she had
ever known before. But most cradle Catholics she spoke to
were a bit oblivious to what the mystery means for us and our
lives. Though in some sense they believed in the Trinity, and
even made the sign of the cross every day, it was not obvious to
them that the Trinity is the purpose of life and the reason for
the world. Whether we are cradle Catholics or converts, this
connection may be new to some of us too. Perhaps we have
never thought or heard of any connection between the purpose question and the mystery of the Trinity. Perhaps no one

has ever explained that you and I *can* enter the Holy Trinity or *how* anyone might do so. It is high time, however, for Catholics to hear this good news and learn how to enter that bright place.

Even when we hear the point clearly, though, it may not initially sound very fulfilling. It might sound abstract and rather removed from real life. Some might object: "You say nothing could be better than knowing, loving, and enjoying the Holy Trinity, but I can think of many things a lot better than that!" And one might go on to name one or more things from one's package of personally preferred goods.

In response, it is important to say that no one is proposing that the purpose of life is knowing, loving, and enjoying God *instead of* the good things of this world. Rather, the Gospel proposes that knowing, loving, and enjoying God is the *ultimate* purpose of life and the true *center* of the human heart. God has given us the good things of this world—many finite goods—to be secondary in our lives. The secondary goods have their place in a life of participating in the Trinity, but it is not the first place. The primary thing is our relationship with God and the life of knowing, loving, and enjoying him.

Long experience among human beings has shown that when secondary goods take over the first place, our enjoyment of the secondary goods is diminished if not destroyed. When secondary goods are brought into our relationship with God, however, everything else is enhanced. We see these things as gifts and blessings—real reflections of God's wisdom and goodness and love at work in our lives. Sunsets are quite literally more beautiful and more enjoyable for those who enjoy them with God than for those who enjoy

the same sight but without God. And the same holds for every other good of this world. Everything in life is better when we receive it from God, on his terms, with gratitude, and return it to him with joy.

A Window into Heaven

Even with all that has been said so far, to ponder the Trinity as the purpose of life, and to see our lives in view of this, may still sound a bit abstract. So, let us take a moment to meditate on the mystery of the Trinity in a more concrete way by taking a look at the famous Russian icon of the Trinity by Andrei Rublev.

In the icon everything is symbolic. In a way, it contains the whole Gospel in symbolic form, so let us go through its symbolism.

The icon as a whole depicts an event in the Old Testament in which three strangers visit Abraham and he shows them hospitality (see Gen 18:1–8). The New Testament, according to a traditional interpretation, says the strangers were angels (see Heb 13:2). The Fathers of the Church saw in the visitation of the angels and the hospitality of Abraham a prefiguration of the Holy Trinity. So, Rublev depicts three angels in the icon, and the angels stand for the Persons of the Holy Trinity.

The three angels are seated in a perfect circle.

Because a circle is without beginning and without end, it is the universal symbol of eternity, for eternity is Life without beginning or end. By depicting the angels within a circle, the icon reveals that the life of the Trinity is eternal. The Trinity does not change. As it was in the beginning, it is now, and ever shall be.

Another detail to notice is the colors of the garments on the angels. Each has a garment with a distinctive color, but they also all have one color in common. The common color is blue, which in Eastern iconography symbolizes divinity. The distinctive colors make the point that each of them is a distinct Person in God, while the common color blue demonstrates that each Person is simply God: they are equal in divinity.

The angel on the right wears a green garment. Green conjures up images of springtime and is the universal symbol for life. In the Nicene Creed, we profess the Holy Spirit to be the Lord, the Giver of Life. So, the angel on the right symbolizes the Holy Spirit.

The angel in the middle wears an earthy brown color. Earthy brown is fitting for someone who walked the earth, and so the middle angel represents the Person who became Incarnate for us: Jesus of Nazareth, who is the eternal Son of God. The gold band on his shoulder represents kingship. Jesus of Nazareth is the King of the Universe, and when he came he proclaimed "the kingdom of God is at hand" (Mk 1:15). Another thing to notice is his right hand. He extends two fingers, and the two fingers are a proclamation of the two natures of Jesus: human and divine. Jesus is the God-Man.

The angel on the left wears an ethereal color hard to name. Even after the incarnation, the eternal Father remains very mysterious to us. Thus, the angel on the left represents the Father. The other two angels bow their heads toward him. This signifies their full acknowledgment of the Father, who is their origin without origin. Yet all three Persons are nonetheless coequal and coeternal, as the icon's circular form shows. It is also clear that the other two angels are making eye contact with him. They know him. And their eye contact with him is the sign of thoroughgoing knowledge, relationship, and the freedom to be who one is with the Father.

In the mysterious life of the Holy Trinity, all is light, love, life, freedom, and enjoyment without beginning and without end. It is rather impossible for us to fathom what such an existence would be, but the point of our life is to find out. Indeed, the point of our life is to enter into this most amazing Life beyond all others, to participate in it for all eternity, and to enjoy the Father, Son, and Holy Spirit. That is why God made human beings. The reason God made the world of nature was to serve us on our journey into the Trinity, so the images around and behind the angels in the icon are also revealing.

Behind the Holy Spirit is a mountain. In Scripture, great things happen on mountains. The Old Law was given on Mount Sinai; the New Law was given in the Sermon on the Mount. On Mount Tabor, the voice of the Father and the cloud of the Holy Spirit revealed the eternal Sonship of Jesus in the Transfiguration (see Mt 17:1–8). The Spirit plays a marvelous role in our lives too. As we will see in later chapters, the Spirit unites us to the Son and leads us to the Father.

Behind the eternal Son is a tree. It was by eating the fruit of a tree that the human race first fell from grace in the Garden of Eden (see Gen 3). It was on the tree of the Cross that the Lord Jesus saved the human race by offering himself in sacrifice for sin (see Is 53:10). And in the new and heavenly Jerusalem stands the tree of life whose leaves are medicine for the healing of the nations (see Rev 22:1–2). In every Mass, when we receive Holy Communion, we eat the fruits of the life-giving tree—the cross of Christ—in order to be saved from the effects of the death-dealing one—the tree of disobedience from which the first humans ate.

Behind the Father is a house. It reminds us of the words of the Lord: "In my Father's house are many rooms" (Jn 14:2). Through his resurrection, Jesus has gone to the Father's house to prepare a place for us to abide in God for eternity. The house, too, is a sign of welcome. It signifies the peace of heart, the simplicity, and the joy of being at home after a long journey in a strange land. In the Father's house, in the heavenly places, each of us is awaited—each of us is loved (see Benedict XVI, *Spe Salvi*, no. 3).

The icon also offers a teaching on the Eucharist, but the way it does so is mysterious. In fact, it does so in two ways, one more obvious and another more hidden. First, on the altar there is a bowl with a bull's head on it. This is a sign of sacrifice according to the rites of the Old Testament. Those rites are once and for all fulfilled in the New Testament when Jesus offered himself in sacrifice on the cross. Second, in a more hidden way, if one looks at the icon with care, it is possible to see how the whole altar itself takes the shape of a chalice and Jesus is in the chalice. The point is that the Eucharist is the real presence of Jesus Christ—body, blood, soul, and divinity. His sacrifice is not far from each of us but is present on the altar at Mass (or, as the Eastern tradition calls it, the Divine Liturgy). What is offered on the altars is not a second sacrifice, but one and the same as that of Jesus on Good Friday. Thus, the medicine of the tree of life is at hand. We will continue to read more on the Eucharist in later chapters, and on how essential it is for us to live into the Trinity.

One might be wondering, at this point, how all of this actually relates to you and me. So, let us notice one last thing. In the front of the icon, at the base of the altar, there is an opening to the viewer. The opening exercises a silent influence on the viewer, drawing us in. The whole scene is open, inviting, attractive. The point is that the Holy Trinity is now calling us—every human being on the face of the earth—to participation in the most amazing and awe-inspiring life of the Father, Son, and Holy Spirit. It pleases the Trinity to be the great joy of our hearts.

The big question now is practical. If the purpose of our lives is to participate in the Holy Trinity, what is the *way* into the Trinity? *How* does anyone enter? We shall speak to the practical question over the remaining chapters.

CHAPTER TWO

To Be Jesus Christ

IN TODAY'S WORLD, a particularly hot topic in virtually every domain of life is identity. The many conversations around this topic speak to the second great question every human being carries in the depths of his or her heart: the identity question—*Who am I*? Like the purpose question, the identity question is one of the most important and profound that anyone can ask. The answer one gives (or receives) is at the core of one's sense of self, worth, meaning, and orientation in life. At the center of every human person, the answer to the identity question is like a personal compass. The answer points out the way to go in the middle of complex and changing circumstances. Yet, in today's world, many people are not clear on how to answer the question. In this chapter, after considering some common ways our world approaches the question,

we will consider the answer according to the Gospel. The
Gospel answer, as we shall see, is amazing.

God Speaks to the Identity Question

It is clear enough how many people *try* to answer the
identity question. Nearly everything in the world has been
tried as a source of identity: family background, ethnic heri-
tage, racial group, social class, financial status, educational
level, professional occupation, personal relationships, sexual
orientation, gender, activisms of every sort whether social or
political, grand schemes to transform the world, ideological
commitments and projects (feminism, environmentalism,
etc.), various religious groups, physical fitness associations,
online communities, and even absorption in pets, gardens,
hobbies, and the petty affairs of life—including Church life.
The list goes on and on. Let us call all such matters, all things
less than God himself, "things under the sun." The question is
whether anything under the sun, or any combination package
of things under the sun, could ever be the whole truth of a
person's identity. Could anything under the sun ever be the
complete answer to the question of who someone is?

The answer of Scripture is no. People often wonder why the
book of Ecclesiastes is in the Bible. At first glance, it seems to
have many dark sayings, such as "All is vanity and a striving after
wind" (Eccles 1:14). Since all Scripture is inspired by God, how
could God say such a thing? But in this book God does something wonderful. God knows well of the many philosophies of
human beings who seek to find their purpose and their identity
in terms of all the things under the sun rather than looking to

him to reveal it, and in Ecclesiastes God offers his commentary on all such philosophies and identity projects.

The author of the book is a sage of Israel who speaks in the voice of someone who "had it all." In his story, once upon a time he was the king of Israel. He accumulated massive riches to the point of having "silver and gold and the treasure of kings and provinces; I got singers, both men and women, and many concubines, man's delight" (Eccles 2:8). He also had faith in God, and believed God gave Israel the covenants and the law. Yet over the course of the book, his meditation crystallizes into a certain line of reasoning. Given the conditions in which we find ourselves in this broken world, *if* the only things available to human beings are the things under the sun, and *if* we must find our purpose and build our identities merely out of the things under the sun, and *if* God offers us nothing more than this world, then ultimately "all is vanity and a chasing after wind."

In the book of Ecclesiastes, God offers a sort of commentary on that line of reasoning. Basically, God agrees that *if* the only things available to us are the things under the sun, and *if* we as humans must find our purpose and identity only in those things, and *if* God offers us nothing more than this world, then indeed it follows: "All is vanity and a striving after wind." The big question is whether all the *ifs* are true. To that question, God answers no. Through Scripture as a whole, in fact, God tells there is much more to our identity and far more to our purpose than all the things under the sun. God wants to give us something more than the world.

The true answer will not be found in looking only to the things of this world, but in looking to God in Jesus Christ.

One of Pope Saint John Paul II's favorite sayings was that "Christ fully reveals man to man himself."[2] The statement makes an amazing point about all human beings, male and female. The point is not primarily about *what* a human being is, but *who* God created you and me and all of us together to be. It is not so much about our essence but about our identity. Let us try to unpack the point in more detail.

The essence of a thing is what it is, or its nature. Human reason, sound philosophy, and common sense can know the essence or nature of many things at least to some extent. For example, we can know that all human beings belong to one universal order of justice, that all human beings can know the order of justice to *some* extent, and that all human beings are subject to it. One need not be Christian to recognize the reality of a higher law. The Nuremberg trials are a good example. The verdicts handed down in those trials rest on several bases. First, there is a higher law transcending all human systems of law. The higher law is the truth that there is a difference between good and evil, right and wrong, and the higher law includes the truths about which things are good and which things are evil. Second, it is possible for all human beings to know the higher law at least to *some* extent regardless of the civic laws of their society, their cultural background, or their religious affiliation. Third, the higher law governs all humanity—especially all the rulers and law-makers of all societies. All are bound to obey it regardless of

---

2. Second Vatican Council, *Gaudium et Spes*, The Holy See, December 7, 1965, no. 22, https://www.vatican.va/archive/hist_councils/ii_vatican_council/documents/vat-ii_const_19651207_gaudium-et-spes_en.html.

the civic laws of their specific times and places. In the Nuremberg trials, the verdicts handed down were based on the reality and knowability of the universal higher law. We can see from this that *what* human beings are in essence, and what is good for us as humans, is a matter at least somewhat accessible to human reason and common sense.[3]

To know *who* a human being is, however, is another matter. One can know that Peter is a human being, for example, and even know what a human is more generally, but without really knowing who *Peter* is at all. Who is Peter? That is the identity question, and our ability to understand something of human nature in general does not fully answer the identity question for any one or all of us. Rather, God alone knows the whole answer to the identity question for each and all of us, and God has revealed the answer to us in Jesus Christ. "Jesus Christ fully reveals man to man himself" means that Jesus Christ is *who* God created you and me and all human beings to be. God is now calling each one and all of us to become and to be Jesus Christ.

Becoming Jesus through Baptism

The announcement that you and I are called to become Jesus Christ is astonishing, and upon first hearing it we might be tempted to interpret the statement metaphorically. But

---

3. More recently, the appeal to the reality of a higher law rationally accessible to all people was an essential part of the argument behind desegregation and the civil rights movement of the 1960s. See Martin Luther King Jr., "Letter from Birmingham Jail."

that would be a serious misinterpretation. It would funda-
mentally miss the point of the Gospel. God is calling you and
me to a union and identification with Jesus so real and so radical it changes us to the core. Such a union and identification
with him can only come about by grace and, more specifically,
by the grace of Baptism. The grace of Baptism transforms our
very identities.

The transformation of our identity by grace is much
greater than most people suspect at first, so let us ponder the
mystery a bit. The place to begin is the Baptism of the Lord.
In his Baptism, something great took place that reveals what
takes place in ours. The Baptism of the Lord reveals the mystery, the meaning, and the magnitude of our own Baptism.
His Baptism reveals what Baptism works in us by grace, who
we are now, and who we can become more and more.

According to the Gospel of Mark, after John baptized
Jesus in the Jordan, Jesus came up out of the water, the
heavens opened, the Spirit descended like a dove, and a voice
was heard from heaven saying: "You are my beloved Son;
with you I am well pleased" (Mk 1:10–11 NABRE). Here all
three divine Persons are revealed. The dove signifies the
Spirit, the voice signifies the Father, and the Father reveals
the true identity of Jesus: "You are my beloved Son." Those
simple words reveal the most profound and world-trans-
forming truth ever spoken. Jesus of Nazareth is the eternal
Son of God.

As the eternal Son, his is a life of relations within the
Trinity. He is the Son of the Father. He breathes the Spirit of
Love. In our Baptism, Christ takes us into his life of relations

within the inner life of God. His relations become ours *by grace*. We begin to participate in them. His Father becomes our Father. His Spirit becomes our Spirit. You and I become one with the eternal Son of God by grace. It is worth pondering such things more, because few Catholics realize the full magnitude of what it means to be baptized.

Scripture says that whoever is baptized is "baptized into Christ" (Rom 6:3; Gal 3:27). What does that mean? It means that whoever is baptized becomes Christ. That is why Baptism was traditionally called *christening*. In the sacrament, the living Lord Jesus transmits or channels to you and me a share in his personal identity. The eternal Son of God stamps and seals into the depths of our souls something of *who* he is. The implication is radical. As a result of Baptism, *you are Jesus*. Each baptized person can say: *I am Jesus*. Although distinctions need to be drawn about what that means, and in due course we will draw them, it is not just a metaphor. For in our Baptism each of us receives in the depths of our souls a sacramental seal, an indelible character, a true share in who Jesus is.

Additionally, all who are baptized receive a new form of life surging through them: the life of grace. The new life of grace is not just "more life" of the natural order. It is a form of life not of this world. The life of grace is *beyond* all of the natures or essence of all finite beings whatsoever—even beyond the nature of the angels. It is life on a whole new level—on a supernatural level. The new life of grace is a real sharing in the *divine Life* of Jesus Christ himself. Those who are baptized and living in the state of grace, though still living on the earth, also live something of the life of heaven. Even now, in the depths of our souls, we participate by grace in the life of the Holy Trinity.[4] We have taken up the position of the eternal Son within the Trinity, so to speak, and live *something* of his own relation to the Father. You are Jesus by the grace of adoption, we say, and, provided you do not throw away the gift of grace by mortal sin without repentance, you will live his divine Life forevermore.

Certain sins are called *mortal* because they kill the life of grace given to the soul in Baptism (see 1 Jn 5:16). A mortal sin is a deliberate free choice of something gravely evil. A person commits a mortal sin when he or she knows a certain act is gravely evil, yet freely and deliberately chooses to carry it out nonetheless. Doing so forms in the heart of the person a condition of *aversion from God*.[5] The aversion from God remains unless there is an actual change of heart. The change of heart from the former choice of sin to a new love for God above all things is called *repentance*. Repentance, in its most basic sense, consists of sorrow for sins committed and a firm resolution to sin no more with the help of God's grace. Thankfully, the God of merciful love has given us the sacrament of Penance in order to restore the life of grace to the soul when it has been lost after Baptism due to sin. The sacrament also renews the life of grace even when it has not been lost but simply weakened by lesser sins.

---

4. In a sense, our bodies also participate in the life of the Trinity by the overflow of grace from soul, but in quite a limited way so long as we are still in this life.

5. Saint Thomas Aquinas, *Summa Theologiae* I–II, q. 87, a. 4, resp.

Naturally, people might wonder which sins are mortal sins. A complete answer to the question requires a good moral catechesis, but a good place to start is a solid and approved examination of conscience.[6] A good examination of conscience is not only crucial to making a good confession, but for many people it can serve as a sort of crash course in matters of serious sin. Learning the truth about sin in order to avoid it is essential for living the life of grace given to us in Baptism, as well as for growing in union with the Lord Jesus more and more.

Growing in Union with Jesus

When Jesus calls us to follow him, and become his disciples, he calls us to something much more radical than first meets the eye. Whether we are baptized as infants or as adults, the following of Jesus Christ in discipleship means waking up more and more to what is given to us in Baptism. It is about learning more and more what it means to be Jesus by grace, accepting his identity more and more as our own, and living more and more as another Christ in this world. In order to receive more deeply the grace of union and identification with Jesus, to live his divine Life more consciously and freely, we must listen to the Teacher.

In the Gospels, people often call Jesus by the title of "the Teacher." The Teacher and his teachings are different from

---

6. For a brief guide to confession and an examination of conscience, see Fr. Bill Murphy, *Basic Helps to Confession* (Boston: Pauline Books and Media, 2000).

every other teacher for a special reason. Other teachers and
their teachings seek to inform and explain. Jesus does so too,
but his words and teachings are much more than bullet
points in a classroom. Bullet points inform us but are otherwise passive. The words and teachings of Jesus, however, are
active. They bear a certain supernatural energy or working
power in them (see Heb 4:12). The goal of the Teacher is not
simply to inform us but rather to transform us, and in a way
beyond what any other teacher or teaching can do. His goal
is *to identify us with himself.* His words, his teachings, and his
deeds work inwardly in our hearts to bring about our identification with him. They supernaturally summon us to follow
the Teacher and to be "doers of the word, and not hearers
only" (Jas 1:22). Those who do so come to live his very Life.

The Teacher himself said so. "I am the vine, you are the
branches" (Jn 15:5). A vine and its branches are one whole
organism and one life. All the life, sap, nutrients, and energy
of the vine flow into the branches. Jesus and the baptized are
one whole organism and one life. You and I are branches on
the vine of Christ. The divine Life of Jesus, his working
power or energy, flows into the depths of our souls and ani-
mates our very being. For thanks to Baptism, and the gift of
sanctifying grace, we are his body parts in the world in a mysterious but real way. Such a close union with Jesus is impossible to fathom, but Jesus revealed it clearly to Saint Paul:
"Saul, Saul, why are you persecuting *me*?" (Acts 9:4 NABRE,
emphasis added). The words of the risen Lord revealed to
Saul just how *one* Christ and the Christian people really are,
and how Saul was persecuting Jesus Christ himself in the
flesh of Christ's people.

After his conversion and Baptism, Saul came to be known as Paul. The name change symbolized the transformation of his identity. The transformation of his self-understanding, too, was so radical that Saint Paul would later exclaim: "It is no longer I who live, but Christ who lives in me" (Gal 2:20). By the time he wrote these words, Paul had profoundly internalized the lessons of the revelation he received on the road to Damascus. The source of life animating him was no longer just his own human soul, but the grace and life of Jesus Christ himself at work in the depths of his soul. Paul had become deeply aware that his true identity was to be Jesus, to live as Jesus, to walk as Jesus, to suffer as Jesus, and to die as Jesus.

The saints in every age demonstrate a similarly radical identification with Jesus. One recent example is a French saint of the early twentieth century, Elizabeth of the Trinity. Her beautiful *Prayer to the Holy Trinity* addresses different stanzas to different Persons of the Trinity. In her prayer to Jesus, she says:

> But I feel my weakness, and I ask you to "clothe me with yourself," to identify my soul with all the movements of your Soul, to overwhelm me, to possess me, to substitute yourself for me that my life may be but a radiance of your Life.[7]

It is clear that she wanted to get out of the way of Christ living in her. She wanted to become wholly identified with him, and simply allow him to live through her human nature.

---

7. *The Complete Works of Elizabeth of the Trinity*, ed. Conrad de Meester, O.C.D., vol. 1, *I Have Found God*, trans. Sister Aletheia Kane, O.C.D. (Washington, DC: ICS Publications, 1984), 183.

A few stanzas later, in addressing the Holy Spirit, she prays in even clearer and more radical terms to be Jesus:

> Consuming Fire, Spirit of Love, "come upon me," and create in my soul a kind of incarnation of the Word: that I may be another humanity for Him in which He can renew his whole mystery.[8]

If Saint Elizabeth could become aware of such mysteries of union with the Lord, and ask for such radical things as for him to renew his incarnation in her, then we should ask for such things too. God is a generous giver, and he will hear our prayer. "Ask and it will be given to you; seek and you will find; knock and the door will be opened to you" (Mt 7:7 NABRE).

Radiating Christ

Now, when we hear about union and identification with Jesus in such radical terms, when we hear *you are Jesus*, that this is not a mere metaphor, and that many saints even pray to become Jesus more and more, many hesitations and difficulties normally arise. We can struggle to believe it or to accept our baptismal identity. Let us consider some common reasons people hesitate, and make some clarifications.

Some people are rightly worried that identification with Jesus means being absorbed into Jesus like a drop of water blends into the ocean. If I become Jesus, do I as a person just vanish or disappear? No. Down through the centuries, various pagan groups or philosophical schools have offered

---

8. *The Complete Works of Elizabeth of the Trinity*, 183.

"absorption" accounts of union with God. What distinguishes a Christian understanding of union with God from all of the others is precisely the point that in the Christian account we are *not* absorbed into God. Rather, just as the three persons of the Trinity remain distinct within the one divine life of God, so we too remain distinct persons when we come to share in the life of the Trinity by grace.

The concern about absorption serves to clarify the nature of our union and identification with Jesus. When God unites us to himself by grace, our distinct personhood is not obliterated but becomes permeated by the divine Light, Love, and Life of the eternal Son. Those who are baptized and living in a state of grace are a bit like Jesus Christ in the transfiguration. His human nature was certainly there in the Transfiguration, but the divine Sonship irradiated his humanity from the depths of his being. Similarly, after baptism our human nature and our distinct human personalities remain, but something of the divinity of Jesus Christ is now present in us and shining from the depths of our souls. When God looks at us, he sees it all: our human nature, our human personalities, and "Christ in you" (Col 1:27). Such is the beauty of our true identity in Jesus Christ. By grace each of us is a distinct branch on the Vine, but all live the same life of the Vine. Each of us takes up our unique place within the whole mystical body of Christ without ceasing to be distinct persons within the whole. Scripture has a name for this wonderful sort of union-without-absorption. It is called *communio*. *Communio* is the mystery of many distinct persons participating in one common divine Life by grace (see 1 Jn 1:3). We shall say more about it in the next chapter.

Perhaps a bigger reservation when hearing *you are Jesus*, however, is the felt sense of being so different from Jesus. We often feel unlike him in so many ways in our thoughts, words, and actions. Jesus is completely holy, and we are sinners in many ways. It is perhaps easy to affirm that you and I are *called* to be Jesus—somehow, someway, someday. But it is hard to affirm you and I *already are* Jesus to some extent— even now. It was precisely in response to this common struggle that Pope Saint John Paul II taught: "We are not the sum of our weaknesses and failures, we are the sum of the Father's love for us and our real capacity to become the image of His Son Jesus."[9]

All who are baptized have received an amazing grace. Thanks to Baptism, you are already Jesus in some ways but not yet Jesus in others. You and I are called to grow into being Jesus more and more. True, no Christian on earth is already fully grown into "the stature of the fullness of Christ" (Eph 4:13). But, thanks to Baptism, the reality of being Jesus has already begun in our souls by grace. Even now, though we are still on the way to being fully grown, Jesus Christ shines out of Christians in certain ways. I never met Mother Teresa, but I know many who did. Every one of them can attest that her whole being radiated Christ in ways palpable to everyone around her. As soon as she walked into the room, they say, one

---

9. Saint John Paul II, Homily for World Youth Day, The Holy See, July 28, 2002, no. 5, https://www.vatican.va/content/john-paul-ii/en/homilies/2002/documents/hf_jp-ii_hom_20020728_xvii-wyd.html. For John Paul II, "to become the image of his Son" is to be Jesus in the sense we have sketched out over the course of the chapter.

could feel the Presence coming from her. But one need not be a canonizable saint to radiate Christ.

Several years ago, I visited a college campus in the midwestern United States. I spent some time at the Catholic campus ministry preaching, celebrating the sacraments, and meeting with students individually. One student who signed up to meet with me was a regular at the campus ministry and spent most of his free time hanging out there, studying or socializing. When I met with him, I learned he was not a Catholic and not even a Christian. He had not been raised with any particular faith. So I said to him, "I have to ask you a question. There are many other places on campus you could go, and many other student organizations you could join, but you choose to come and spend your time here. If you are not a Catholic, why do you hang out *here* rather than elsewhere?" "I do not know," he replied, "there is just something different about these people." When I asked him to say more, he was at a loss for words. He just repeated, "I don't know, they are just different from everyone else." Obviously, he sensed something different, something magnetic, in otherwise ordinary students. It was enough to captivate his attention and keep him hanging out around the campus ministry. I do not blame the young man for having no words for it. Supernatural mysteries are hard to put into words, and without the Scriptures and tradition to guide us no one can really do it. Perhaps the only way to describe what he experienced is to say he sensed something of the kindly light of "Christ in you."

Mother Teresa's sisters, the Missionaries of Charity, have the custom of reciting a certain prayer every day after Mass. It is called "Radiating Christ," and the prayer summarizes perfectly what can become of all who are baptized, who live in grace, and who identify with Jesus. Let us close this chapter with the prayer.

> Dear Jesus, help us to spread Your fragrance everywhere we go. Flood our souls with Your spirit and life. Penetrate and possess our whole being so utterly that our lives may only be a radiance of Yours. Shine through us and be so in us that every soul we come in contact with may feel Your presence in our souls. Let them look up and see no longer us but only Jesus! Stay with us and then we shall begin to shine as You shine, so to shine as to be a light to others; the light, O Jesus, will be all from You; none of it will be ours: it will be You shining on others through us. So let us thus praise You in the way You love best: by shining on those around us. Let us preach You without preaching, not by words, but by our example, by the catching force, the sympathetic influence of what we do, the evident fullness of the love our hearts bear to You. Amen.[10]

---

10. "Radiating Christ" was adapted from the original prayer written by Saint John Henry Newman in his book, *Meditations and Devotions*.

CHAPTER THREE

The Spirit of Love

"THE SINGLE DESIRE that dominated my search for delight was simply to love and to be loved," said Saint Augustine.[11] In these words, he spoke for every human being. Our whole sense of fulfillment and happiness is bound up with love. Human beings are programmed for relationship. More than a century of psychological studies has shown that children who are deprived of love in significant ways inevitably develop psychological disorders. The more profound is the lack of love, the more profound are the disorders.[12] A vast

---

11. Saint Augustine, *Confessions*, II.ii.2, 24.

12. Charles A. Nelson, Nathan A. Fox, and Charles H. Zeanah, *Romania's Abandoned Children: Deprivation, Brain Development, and the Struggle for Recovery* (Cambridge, MA, and London: Harvard University Press, 2014). The topic belongs to the field of attachment theory. For a thorough overview of the field, see Jude Cassidy and Phillip R. Shaver, eds., *Handbook of*

body of research also shows that human beings have an innate felt need to *belong*, and people who lack a sense of belonging also tend to suffer from a variety of disorders.[13] Pope Saint John Paul II spoke an eternal truth when he said:

> Man cannot live without love. He remains a being that is incomprehensible for himself, his life is senseless, if love is not revealed to him, if he does not encounter love, if he does not experience it and make it his own, if he does not participate intimately in it.[14]

The love question, therefore, is a most essential one. It is really a cluster of many questions. How do I find love? Who am I going to love and who am I going to let love me? How will I give and receive love? Again, we find amazing answers to these questions in the Gospel of Jesus Christ.

The Gift of Love

God himself knows our radical need for love. He placed the thirst for love into our hearts in order to slake it. In the Gospel of John, when the Lord Jesus met the woman at the

---

Attachment, 3rd. ed. (New York & London: The Guilford Press, 2016). Conrad Baars and Anna Terruwe also speak extensively to the question. See their book *Healing the Unaffirmed: Recognizing Emotional Deprivation Disorder* (Staten Island, NY: Alba House, 2002).

13. Two pioneers of research on belonging were R. F. Baumeister & M.R. Leary. See "The need to belong: Desire for interpersonal attachments as a fundamental human motivation," *Psychological Bulletin* 117, no. 3 (1995): 497–529.

14. Pope Saint John Paul II, *Redemptor Hominis*, The Holy See, March 4, 1979, no. 22, https://www.vatican.va/content/john-paul-ii/en/encyclicals/documents/hf_jp-ii_enc_04031979_redemptor-hominis.html.

well, he offered her a new kind of drink: living water (see Jn 4:10). He knew she was thirsty for love and had suffered many disappointments in her quest to find it, but the living water he had to give would never leave her thirsty again (see Jn 4:14).

So, too, it is with you and me. Over the course of our lives, you and I become familiar with many forms of love. In one way or another, we experience the love of parents for their children, the love of children for their parents, and the love of friends and peers growing up. We might see in others, and perhaps experience for ourselves, romantic love and relationships. Romantic love inevitably raises the question of spousal love, marriage, and the promise of permanent or abiding love. Spousal love essentially means children and family—a truth often forgotten or opposed in various ways in our society. Spousal love exercises the greatest appeal to our hearts, but there are other forms of love too. Soldiers who endure combat together, for example, forge a unique bond of love with one another. They become a "band of brothers." To a lesser degree, something similar happens to firefighters, intensive care doctors and nurses, and even college students who live and work together in close quarters for years. All such forms of love are natural. Each of them is good and has its satisfactions— sometimes very deep satisfactions. No matter how good each or all of them might be, however, they all point to something more. For loves of the natural variety are one and all *finite*. Every one of them is limited in various ways and inevitably leaves something to be desired.

The living water from the Lord Jesus, however, is different. It is the one thing that quenches completely the thirst

for love. For the living water he has to give is not one of the
forms of natural love with which we are familiar from our
ordinary experience. It is not of this world. It is, rather, the
Holy Spirit himself. The Holy Spirit is the eternal breath of
love between the Father and the Son. From all eternity the
Father and the Son behold each other in a mutual and eternal
look of love. The Father and the Son breathe a sigh of love
for one another without ceasing, and their eternal sigh of
love is the Spirit of Love. The Spirit of Love is nothing less
than a divine Person proceeding from the Father and the
Son. The good news is that it has pleased God to share his
Spirit of Love personally with us.

For the Father has sent his eternal Son Jesus Christ into
the world. Jesus freely chose to die on the cross for you and
me, but death could not hold him. God raised him from the
dead, and now he lives to die no more. Day and night the
Lord Jesus stands before the Father in the heavenly places and
pleads for us to receive the outpouring of the Spirit. In answer
to the prayer of the Son, the Father indeed lavishes the Spirit
upon us at Pentecost. One of the most amazing and life-
transforming announcements anyone could ever hear is that
"the love of God has been poured forth in our hearts through
the Holy Spirit who has been given to us" (Rom 5:5).[15]

These words of Saint Paul are much more astounding
than anyone might realize at first. In one way, the Holy Spirit
is universally present and active in all things and in all people.
For God is present always and everywhere inasmuch as he

---

15. Translation by author.

creates each and every person and thing of nature. Truly, the Holy Spirit gives being, life, breath, activity, and every blessing of nature to all in the world of creation. One common prayer of the Byzantine liturgy calls upon the Spirit, saying, "you who are everywhere present and fill all things." The words of the prayer are an echo of Scripture: "the Spirit of the Lord has filled the world" (Wis 1:7). For never has a star moved across the night sky or a blade of grass grown up on the earth or a human being come into this world unless the Holy Spirit was present and at work in the process.

Saint Paul's words about the Spirit of Love poured into our hearts, however, tell us of something more—something different—from the common presence of the Spirit who fills all things in creating them. Thanks to the death and resurrection of Jesus, the Father has sent the Spirit of Love into our hearts in a new, distinct, and special way. In this new and special way, the Spirit comes not only to create us but *to save us*. When the Spirit comes into our souls on his mission to save, he comes to accomplish in us something greater—something over and above—the creation of the whole world of nature. The Spirit comes to transform us into the personal friends of God.

Becoming a Friend of God

In our society, Christianity is widespread enough that many people have heard of having a personal relationship with Jesus. It is so common to hear of it, in fact, that one might get the impression it is a normal or natural thing to do—to be personal friends with God. But it is not. To be personal friends with God is rather beyond all the powers of our human nature. It is simply impossible for you or me to rise up by our own natural strength and establish ourselves in a personal relationship or friendship with God. For God "dwells in unapproachable light" (1 Tim 6:16). As far as our natural abilities go, therefore, to become the intimate friends and companions of God is simply beyond us. It would be easier for us to jump over the moon.

It is not, however, beyond the *power of God* to make us his friends. Indeed, God has planned to do so from before the foundation of the world. In order to accomplish his purpose of befriending us to himself, God first of all created the world. Just to create things is a gratuitous gift of his love, but it is a gift given commonly to all persons and all things in nature. All the blessings of nature flow from God. Yet God has another gratuitous gift of love to give, a special gift distinct from all the blessings of nature, and the special gift is reserved for persons. Thanks to the death and resurrection of Jesus Christ, God sends the Holy Spirit into our hearts to accomplish in us something that is otherwise impossible for us to do on our own by our natural strength. The Spirit comes to establish us in a personal friendship with God. No created person has a natural right to become personal friends with God. Such a gift is undeserved. It could only be a special favor—a grace. Yet, just because God is good and loves us *excessively*, your soul is now the mission territory of the Spirit.

When the Spirit comes to befriend us to God, the Spirit carries out his work in us gradually and by stages. We do not necessarily experience his presence at first. In fact, most often people are initially unaware of his work in their hearts. The Spirit blows where he wills, and he normally sneaks into our hearts quietly—usually too quietly for us to notice at first. But though one might be oblivious to the Spirit of Love at work in the depths of one's heart, the Spirit is active nonetheless. One cannot say that every human being is in a state of sanctifying grace, but there is no one on earth who is untouched by the grace of the Holy Spirit. The grace of the Spirit and his work in the soul take different forms and modes in different people, depending on where they are in the journey of their conversion and spiritual development.

Although there is a great deal of variety and particularity in how the Spirit works in different people, one can nonetheless speak of two general ways. On the one hand, the Spirit touches all human hearts in more or less transitory ways in order to prepare people for something more. On the other hand, the Spirit comes to live and dwell in the heart in a stable and abiding way through Baptism. Generally speaking, the Spirit touches different people at different times and places in different ways in order to prepare them to believe in God, to believe in the gospel of Jesus Christ, and to receive the grace of the indwelling of the Spirit given in Baptism. Sometimes the Spirit's preparatory work is more remote in people's lives and sometimes more proximate, but one way or another, the Spirit works in hearts everywhere to prepare people to receive the grace of conversion and the grace of his indwelling.

In the process of converting us, the Spirit first enters our heart, illuminates the depths of our mind, and makes us interiorly aware—at least vaguely—of the need to change our lives. According to God's designs for each person, the Spirit inclines people to go in search of various things such as forgiveness, healing, freedom, or a new understanding of what life is all about. Many people have told me that the first time they went into a church, or back to church, they had no idea why they were even going. They were just drawn in a way that baffled them. In his work of converting people, the Spirit is like an interior John the Baptist. Just as John the Baptist prepared Israel for the preaching of Jesus, so the Spirit prepares hearts to listen to the testimony of Christian witnesses. Thanks to the preparatory work of the Spirit, hearts are often ready to listen to the good news of Jesus Christ.

In the process of listening, either during or afterward, the Spirit works further in our hearts by lighting up the truthfulness of the Gospel. "Follow me," says the Lord (Jn 1:43). The invitation of the Lord echoes in the deep. Indeed, it echoes from eternity. Though the words "follow me" are heard from without, either through Scripture or Christian witnessing, their truthfulness shines from within, thanks to the light of the Spirit. Many empirically observable signs also confirm the truthfulness of the Gospel: the lives of the saints, the miracles of Christian history, and the peculiar fact of the existence and endurance of the Church over the centuries. The signs are vast in number and kind, and their evidential weight is cumulative. It is possible to investigate and study the signs at length, and many people do. Even when taken all together, however, the signs do not make us see the risen Lord Jesus face to face. The signs serve to distinguish the proclamation of the Gospel from merely human testimony, and help human reason to see how credible the Gospel really is. Rational reflection upon the signs has its place in the process of conversion, but, in the end, we do not believe in the Gospel of Jesus Christ *because* of the many confirmatory signs. Rather, we believe thanks to the light and the call of the Spirit.

The Spirit touches hearts everywhere, in different ways, to prepare people, to convert them to faith, and, if they have not been baptized, to bring them to the waters of Baptism. For in Baptism, the Spirit comes to live and dwell in our hearts in a new way. The grace of Baptism is no transitory touch of the soul; rather, the person of the Spirit himself comes to live and dwell in the soul in a stable way. Our hearts become the home and dwelling place of a most wonderful Guest—the Holy Spirit himself. So long as one lives in a state of grace, the Spirit abides in us. He is available to us personally for knowing and loving. More than anything else, it is his Presence dwelling in our hearts that slakes our thirst for love.

The Communion of Love

Another word for the friendship with God established in us by the Spirit is *communio*. *Communio* came up in the last chapter in order to make a special point. In our Baptism, we receive the grace of union and identification with Jesus Christ. By such grace you and I really do become Jesus Christ, but we are not absorbed into him like a drop of water disappearing into the ocean. Rather, we remain distinct persons. However, at the same time we are also permeated and flooded by his divine Light, Love, and Life in many ways. *Communio* is a great mystery and worth pondering at length. For only in the communion of Love given to us by the Spirit is our felt need for *belonging* ultimately and adequately satisfied.

Communio, as we saw in the last chapter, is the participation of many persons in the one common life of God by grace. The statement is packed with meaning, but it basically means taking your place at the table in the center of the Trinity as we saw in the Rublev icon. When God pours out his Spirit of Love upon us in Baptism, the Spirit comes to live and dwell in our hearts. The Spirit also actively works in our hearts to transform us more and more into Jesus, and ultimately, to turn us toward God the Father. How does all of this take place?

In short, it takes place through the sharing of life. Friends share everything with one another. So, too, in befriending us God shares his life completely with us. God also calls us, in turn, to share our lives completely with him. God first loved us (see 1 Jn 4:19). He sent his Son Jesus into our world to share everything in God with us—all the treasures of the Father's house. The Lord Jesus alone knew the secret of God and the inner life of God as the Holy Trinity. The Lord Jesus alone knew why God created the world. The Lord Jesus alone knew how God had planned all along to draw us into the life of the Trinity by sheer grace. The Father sent Jesus Christ into the world to share the secret with us, and he shared it at the price of his blood shed on the cross. He shared the Word of God with us—his very self—and he shares it with us still in the living words of the prophets and apostles, the inspired Scriptures, and the tradition of the Church.

The Lord Jesus also shares his Spirit with us in our Baptism, in our Confirmation, in every absolution in the sacrament of Penance, and in all the grace of our lives. The Lord shares his Body and Blood with us in the Eucharist. He shares his own mother Mary with us (see Jn 19:27). He shares the lives of all the saints with us. He shares with us the bishops, the priests, and the deacons of the Church. He raises up ministers for our souls and forms them over the course of a lifetime to be of service to us. God has orchestrated all the details of their lives for purposes of their formation—to give us a living word and the blessing of God when we need it the most. Every act of kindness they show us is really from the Lord Jesus himself. So, too, are all the good words and kindly deeds of all the people in the Church who bear the Spirit of the living God in their hearts.[16]

In all of these ways, God shows his love for us and makes it tangible in the Church. The Church is the "home and the school of *communio*."[17] It is the place where friendship with God, both personally and communally, is forged in all of our lives by the power of the Spirit living, dwelling, and working

---

16. It is also important to acknowledge that, in one way or another, all of us also experience the sinfulness of various members of the Church. Many people have been hurt either by ministers or by others in the Church. When we experience love and kindness from the members of the Church, it is a gift and sign of God's love. When we experience sin and hurt from members of the Church, however, it is obviously not from God. As will be explained in Chapter Four, every human being suffers from a certain illness or pathos of the heart and stands in need of healing and renewal by grace. So, too, with all the members of the Church—including the ministers.

17. Pope Saint John Paul II, *Novo Millennio Ineunte*, The Holy See, January 6, 2001, no. 43, https://www.vatican.va/content/john-paul-ii/en/apost_letters/2001/documents/hf_jp-ii_apl_20010106_novo-millennio-ineunte.html.

in our hearts. The Church is the place where you and I hear of *communio* with God, sincerely try to live it, and frequently fail at it, yet also receive forgiveness and a fresh start when we need it. We need a fresh start often. For slowly do we learn the ways of grace. Slowly do we learn how to live and walk in the presence and power of the Spirit. Slowly do we learn to accept the friendship of God in our lives. All of the teachings and all of the practices of the holy Church of God are given to the world so that each of us one and all might go to God—to the Father's house in the heavenly places—on the way of friendship.

The Way of Friendship

All the teachings and practices of the Church together form *the way of friendship*. The way of friendship consists of all the concrete ways and means set before us in the Church for us to take up and use in order to drink deeply of the Spirit, to be transformed into Jesus, and to go home to the Father's house. A good way to understand the way of friendship at first is by comparison with ordinary human friendships. For every good and life-giving element found in ordinary human friendships can also be found on the way of friendship with God in the Church, but in a higher and better way.

Friends live together, speak together, eat together, and work together for good and noble purposes. So, too, on the way of friendship. The Lord Jesus is in our midst. We live with him and encounter him in all the activities of the Church. The Lord speaks to us in Scripture and sacraments, prayer and liturgy, and we speak with him too. The Lord

Jesus touches us in the sacraments by his grace, and in faith we receive and respond to his touch. The Eucharist is our common sacred banquet with God. In the Mass, we offer the Lord's own sacrifice—his Body and Blood—to the Father. To offer the sacrifice is our common work with the Lord Jesus and his Spirit. So, too, is every good and noble effort at the evangelization of the world. For we know that no matter how we might speak to people, all our efforts to evangelize come to nothing unless the Father sends the Spirit into the hearts of people to change them and draw them into *communio* with us.

All of the practices of the Church have their place on the way of friendship with God, and we shall discuss the practicals over the course of the next several chapters. Essentially, the way of friendship is a path of healing and renewal of the human heart, and it all begins with faith and hope in the Lord Jesus. The way of friendship calls us to trust in him and count on his grace. It is also essential to learn his teachings, believe in them, strive to put them into practice, and turn to his mercy when we fail to live accordingly. The more we really accept his grace and truth in our lives, the more we accept his love and really cling to him in love, the more something truly astonishing happens. "All who cling to the Lord become one spirit with him" (1 Cor 6:17).[18]

---

18. Translation by author.

CHAPTER FOUR

The Pathos of the Heart

OVER THE COURSE of years traveling and preaching
everywhere in the United States as well as other coun-
tries, and ministering to thousands of people in many different
personal, social, and cultural situations, it has become clear to
me how difficult it is for virtually all of us to accept the truth
of our baptismal identification with Jesus. Why? We daily
experience the difference between our own hearts and the
heart of Jesus. What goes on in the heart of Jesus is all love and
holiness, but what goes on in our hearts is not. Awareness of
this can make it difficult for any of us to believe in "Christ in
you" (Col 1:27). We commonly lack the traits of the friends of
God and his adopted children: "*parrhesia*,[19] straightforward

---

19. *Parrhesia* is a Greek word that means the ability to speak freely or
boldly. In this context, it means the ability to speak freely with God based on
the confidence that one is accepted and loved.

simplicity, filial trust, joyous assurance, humble boldness, the certainty of being loved" (CCC 2778). Lacking such traits to no small extent, we hesitate to surrender to the mystery. The issue is in the heart.

The human heart stands in need of healing, and the good news is that the grace of healing and transformation of the heart is at hand. Among the most moving prophecies of the Old Testament were God's promises of the day when he would radically renew the hearts of his people (see Ezek 36:26–27), and among the greatest proclamations of the New Testament is the announcement on Pentecost that the promised day has come (see Acts 2:14–36). The Spirit has been poured into our hearts and has set about transforming us (see Rom 5:5). Renewal has begun. Thanks to the grace given to each of us in Baptism, Jesus Christ himself is now the "hidden man of the heart" (1 Pet 3:4),[20] and the divine Life of Jesus is meant to grow in us more and more.

The path to healing is the way of friendship with God in the Church. On the way of friendship, the Holy Spirit dwelling in our hearts is the iconographer who carves the image of Christ deeply within us. As the Spirit does so, the Christian heart becomes increasingly aware of "riches of the glory of this mystery, which is Christ in you" (Col 1:27). The more we grow in awareness and acceptance of this mystery, the more our hearts turn with Jesus and like Jesus to the "Father of lights" (Jas 1:17). Ultimately, our calling is to live under the gaze of the Father who loves us, and to worship him in spirit and in truth (see Jn 4:24). It all begins, however, in the heart.

---

20. Translation by author.

The Mystery of the Human Heart

What is the deepest thing in a human person? Modern science generally, and certain schools of psychology in particular, seek to explain human beings exclusively in mechanistic and materialistic terms. Under their influence, many people now spontaneously think of the depths of their own being in terms of impersonal forces. This leads many people to think that, though we might experience our conscious life as something very personal and rich, at the center of our being the primary factor is either chemical processes, psychic drives, or various sorts of conditioning. Now, it is important to affirm that human beings are physical beings, human beings have psychic drives, and human beings are susceptible to conditioning, but the *primary* factor in the human person is no such impersonal thing. Rather, at the center of the human person is that which is most personal of all—the human heart—and the heart is irreducible to something impersonal. The heart is "the dwelling-place where *I am*" (CCC 2563, emphasis added). Your heart and mine are deeper than all our psychic drives and, in fact, deeper than anything conceptual reason can fathom (CCC 2563). Only God knows what is in a human heart (CCC 2563). It is high time for all of us to think of ourselves and one another in truly human and personal terms. It is time for us to think of human beings primarily in terms of the heart.

Every human being has a heart. The heart is a given of our inner experience. Who would ever want to be called "heartless"? Although we all experience various depths and complexities of the heart every day, our hearts are also hidden from us in many ways. "More tortuous than anything is the human heart, / beyond remedy; who can understand it?" (Jer 17:9 NABRE). Though our hearts are mysterious to ourselves and others, it is possible nonetheless to gain a basic sense of our hearts. Indeed, it is essential to do so.

The way to do so is to ponder the heart in light of other factors in our being. According to the teaching of the Church, a human being is essentially a unit of body and soul. The term *soul*, according to ancient tradition, signifies the source of life in living things, and the presence of soul is what differentiates living organisms from corpses. Our own human souls too are the source of our life in the biological sense. But no small part of the overall life form of human beings is our *inner life* or all the things going on within us: our sensations, images, passions, thoughts, memories, intentions, choices, etc. In its proper sense, the word *heart* signifies the organ beating in our chest and pumping blood, but according to a nearly universal figure of speech the word *heart* also signifies the whole inner life of the human soul. Such is the broadest sense of the word as it is used by biblical authors as well as the Fathers of the Church and the saints and mystics of every age. In this broad sense, Pope Saint John Paul II said that the heart is the "inward mystery of man."[21]

The heart in the broad sense of the term, the inward mystery in each of us, is vast and deep. Each person is, in a sense, a world. Yet it is possible to distinguish different layers of the heart or different regions in the depths of life going on within each of us. The Fathers of the Church sometimes compared our inner life to a church. In every church, there is an area

---

21. Pope Saint John Paul II, *Redemptor Hominis*, no. 8.

where the people gather, called the nave. There is another area where the altar and tabernacle are situated, called the sanctuary. In the nave, people come and go day and night. In the sanctuary, however, the eucharistic Presence remains. So too it is with our inner life. Like the nave, there is a superficial place within us. Just as people come and go in the nave continually, so in this superficial region within us there are sensations, images, and passions that come and go in a fluctuation of impulses and moods and various considerations. Yet there is also a deeper place within us at the center of the soul: the interior sanctuary. Like the sanctuary of a church, in the interior sanctuary at the center of the soul the Presence of God remains day and night. For thanks to Baptism, God dwells in our hearts by grace and is always available for us.[22] He is ever present to us even though we are often not present to him.

In order to say more, certain saints and spiritual writers use more descriptive terms. Saint Diadochos of Photiki calls the interior nave *the area around the heart*.[23] Archimandrite

---

22. A qualification is important: the Presence remains within the interior sanctuary of the soul so long as one is living in a state of grace. Mortal sin destroys the grace of the indwelling, but for those who are baptized, the sacrament of Penance restores it.

23. Saint Diadochos of Photike, "On Spiritual Knowledge and Discrimination" in *The Philokalia*, trans. G.E.H. Palmer, Philip Sherrard, and Kallistos Ware, vol. 1 (New York: Faber & Faber, 1979), 263; *One Hundred Practical Texts of Perception and Spiritual Discernment from Diadochos of Photiki*, trans. Janet Elaine Rutherford (Belfast: Belfast Byzantine Texts and Translations, 2000); "Introductory," St Diadochos of Photiki, Gnostic Chapters, December 24, 2011, http://timiosprodromos8.blogspot.com. The Palmer translation refers to what is within the person but "outside the heart" and the Rutherford translation translates the same expression more literally as "the area around the limbs of the heart."

Zacharias calls the interior sanctuary *the deep heart*.[24] He follows Scripture in doing so (see Ps 64:6 LXX). In the area around the heart, sensations, images, and passions combine and recombine in endless movements of impassioned imagery and automatic reactions to people, circumstances, and events. In the deep heart, however, something more profound is going on. In the deep heart is the awareness of God, spiritual love, conscience, freedom, relationship, prayer, and many more mysteries.

The deep heart of the human person is worth pondering a bit more. In some ways, the spiritual life consists of a pilgrimage to the deep heart. It takes a lifetime to uncover the riches stored up there, and to meet the God who dwells in our hearts thanks to the grace of our Baptism. The deep heart is where you and I are most of all *in the image of God*. The deep heart is able to behold God by grace because it has eyes all of its own, sometimes called the *intellect* or *nous*.[25] The eyes of the heart are an innate ability to know God in a most personal and familiar way, but they require the light of grace to do so. The eyes of the heart were thus made for the contemplation of God—for contemplative prayer in this life and for the unveiled sight of God in the next.[26] The deep heart also has a

---

24. Archimandrite Zacharias, *The Hidden Man of the Heart: The Cultivation of the Heart in Orthodox Christian Anthropology*, ed. Christopher Veniamin (Dalton, PA: Mount Thabor Publishing, 2008), 1.

25. The eyes of the heart are commonly called *intellect* in western theology and *nous* in eastern theology.

26. Contemplative prayer will be discussed in more detail in later chapters.

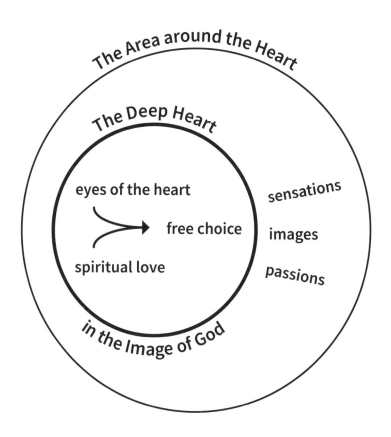

certain capacity for spiritual love, sometimes called the *will*. People often associate the will with *will-power*, but in truth the will is first of all a spiritual hunger of the soul higher than all sensory loves. The deep heart was made to love God above all things. The deep heart also has a first love, whatever it might be. One's first love orients all of one's free choices and acts. Free consent, choices, and other voluntary acts also proceed from the deep heart. So, the *Catechism of the Catholic Church* calls the deep heart "the place of decision . . . where we choose life or death" (CCC 2563).

To love God above all things from the deep heart, freely to live for him as one's first love, is to choose life. To love something other than God more than God, however, freely to set one's heart on something gravely sinful, is to choose death. What and who you and I freely love from the depths of our hearts, and the purpose for which each of us freely lives, determines who each of us will become. You and I answer the purpose question, the love question, and the identity question in the most real and personal ways in the depths of our hearts. For in the depths of the heart you and I answer the questions not only in theory but in practice—in real life choices. Now we might be able to understand better why the *Catechism* says the heart is "the dwelling place where *I* am." The deep heart is where you and I stand at once before God and the whole area around our hearts. It is where you and I can take into consideration the various factors of our being and work out who we are going to be, given all the circumstances of our lives. The big question is whether we will work it all out with God by following Jesus Christ, counting on his grace, and entrusting ourselves to his love and care in the great *communio* of the Church.

The Origins of Our Affliction

When God first created human beings, he created them in his image and likeness. To be made in his image means they had a deep heart in the sense outlined in the previous section, and to say they were in his likeness is to say they knew God very personally and loved him above all other things. For God originally established them in a special state of grace.[27] In the beginning, the souls of the first humans were flooded with grace, and to some extent grace even overflowed into their bodies. As a result of such grace, the first human beings could—in a way—see God in all things around them like so many reflections of light in a mirror. More amazingly still, the eyes of their hearts were so profoundly illuminated by grace that they experienced God personally

---

27. The account of the original condition and fall of human beings laid out in this section and the following is based upon several authorities. First, Saint Thomas Aquinas's summary and synthesis of the Fathers of the Church. *Summa Theologiae* I, qs. 93–102; *Disputed Questions on Truth*, q. 18l; *Compendium of Theology*, c. 186–197. Second, the *Catechism of the Catholic Church*, nos. 355–421 as well as *Christ Our Pascha: Catechism of the Ukrainian Greek Catholic Church* (Kyiv and Edmonton, 2016), nos. 118–177 and 725–801. Third, like the latter sections of *Christ Our Pascha*, it draws its overall vision and inspiration from monastic authors common to the East and West regarding our overall condition as fallen and the purpose of the spiritual journey as one of healing and transformation of the heart where the image of God is primarily to be found in us and renewed by grace. For one example, see Saint John Cassian, *Conferences*, trans. Boniface Ramsey (New York; Newman Press, 1997); Saint Diadochus of Photike, "On Spiritual Knowledge and Discrimination: One Hundred Texts," in *The Philokalia*, trans. and ed. G.E.H. Palmer, Philip Sherrard, and Kallistos Ware, vol. 1 (New York: Faber & Faber, 1979).

and immediately dwelling in their souls. They communicated with God very easily by a special divine inspiration. For them, we can say, God was simply The Presence. Their minds spontaneously interpreted all the things of nature as so many gifts from God, and their passions responded to everything in a perfectly harmonious way. In the beginning, they had no internal emotional conflicts. In their inner life, all was at peace. Prayerfulness was the original condition of the human heart.[28] The first human beings had other forms of knowledge and love too, but all other forms of knowledge and love were integrated into prayerfulness.[29] The first human beings were thus responsible stewards of the things of nature according to divine instructions. In this condition, they knew God, loved God, and enjoyed God. The eyes of their hearts were enlightened by grace. God was their first love and God was their all. Everything else was relative to God. Their whole being, their whole personal world, was organized totally around God.

However, when the first human beings transgressed the commandment of God, they lost the grace in which they were

---

28. Fabio Giardini, O.P. defines prayerfulness as a loving awareness of the presence of God. See his *Prayerfulness: A Psychotheological Search into the Spirit of Prayer* (Pontifical University of Saint Thomas Aquinas, 1984).

29. I say that all other forms of knowledge were integrated into prayerfulness, since they lived in the state of grace and so enjoyed the Spirit's gift of wisdom in some way. Prayerfulness (in Giardini's sense) is essentially the contemplative act of the Spirit's gift of wisdom, and the Spirit's gift of wisdom holds the primacy over theological and philosophical wisdom, and, by implication, all the lower sciences too. See Pope Saint John Paul II, *Fides et Ratio*, no. 44.

created. They largely destroyed the whole arrangement God had established in their being by grace. Instead of seeing the reflection of God in things around them, now they saw just things: plants, animals, sun, moon, stars. Instead of spontaneously interpreting the natural world around them as full of so many gifts from God, now they interpreted everything as merely objects of pleasure and use for themselves. Instead of everything being about God, everything now seemed to be about them.

Interiorly, instead of harmony and peace in their emotional life, now all was riotous and conflicted as their attention turned from worship to survival, from looking to God to looking out for themselves. Instead of experiencing and enjoying the presence of God dwelling in their hearts, they experienced their hearts as empty. The essentials of human nature remained intact, however, so it remained possible to know God in a distant sort of way through philosophical reasoning. But the intimacy with God in the depths of the heart was lost. The eyes of their hearts had become fixated on things in the world, and their first love centered on themselves. By comparison to the original condition in which God created them, their condition was now seriously pathological.

How does all of this affect us? If the first human beings had not sinned, then they would have transmitted to all posterity by way of procreation the original grace and condition in which they had been created. When they fell from grace, however, they could no longer transmit that grace through procreation. As a result, no other human being receives the original grace or original condition of the first humans. We are deprived of the grace and condition of original justice. As a result, what comes down to us instead is their same seriously pathological condition. Let us call it the *pathos of the heart*.

In contemporary English, the term *pathos* means generally an affliction or suffering. In the context of literary studies and drama, it has also come to mean a certain feeling of suffering in an audience member for one of the characters in the story or play. In the context of medicine and therapeutic psychology, it has come to mean an objectively disordered condition—sometimes called a pathological condition. In this book, the expression *pathos of the heart* means the objectively disordered condition of human hearts as a result of the fall. That condition is a true pathological condition, an affliction, and a suffering.

Our commonly inherited pathology does not destroy our human nature or erase the image of God in our deep hearts. Human nature remains the same in its essence. We are still made in the image of God. Yet we no longer inherit from the original human beings the grace they enjoyed in the beginning. We have inherited a universal pathological condition or affliction of the heart, and knowing something of it can help us understand what belongs to our human nature and what belongs to our fallen condition—what we essentially are and what calls for healing and transformation by grace. Understanding the pathos of the heart should evoke from us compassion for ourselves and for all of our fellow human beings. For we are one and all characters in the story of the fall and redemption, and we carry a common set of symptoms.

The Symptoms of Our Affliction

One of the main symptoms of our universally inherited pathology is that all human beings experience a swirl of images and morally disordered passions in the area around the heart. Images and passions combine and recombine in a phenomenon that the ancient monks (and modern ones too) call in Greek *logismoi* (lo-gee-smee). The term translates straightforwardly into English as *thoughts*, but one must be careful not to misunderstand the meaning of the term *thoughts* here. In ordinary English, *thoughts* is a very broad term. It extends to a whole spectrum of good and holy thoughts, neutral thoughts, and morally disordered thoughts. In order to name the symptoms of the pathos of the heart, however, the monks wanted a term not for the good thoughts, or even the neutral thoughts, but specifically for the morally disordered thoughts that commonly come to us. When discussing the problematic end of the spectrum in our thought life, they used the term *logismoi*. In this way, it became something of a technical term for disordered thoughts—impassioned imagery of a morally disordered variety. Such thoughts are initially involuntary, but can become sinful, as we shall explain. Let us begin with examples.

A classic example of *logismoi* is the monk at prayer who has an image of gold pop into his imagination. Now, an image of gold by itself is neutral, but when it triggers *desire* to obtain gold there is a disordered passion associated with the image. The desire is disordered because to seek gold is contrary to the professed state of the monk. Or, in another example, the monk suddenly desires to leave his room during the designated time for prayer to go visit others around the monastery, perhaps in the name of charity or friendliness. In the monastic life, there is a time and place for friendly conversation, but it is not during the period designated for private prayer. The thought of doing so is an example of *logismoi*.

Fallen human beings ordinarily experience all sorts of *logismoi* bombarding us. For example, we might have thoughts such as the following: *Prayer is pointless. If God knows everything, why pray? No one believes this stuff anymore. You are a religious freak. Chastity is impossible; there is no point in trying. If two people love each other, what's wrong with it? Everyone is doing it. It does not matter what you do so long as you do not harm anyone else. You do not need to go to Mass. Skipping Mass on Sundays could not possibly be a mortal sin. Why doesn't God do something about all the evil in the world? You are worthless. No one would ever love you.* And on and on and on. The Fathers of the Church, the saints in every age, and the masters of prayer were well experienced with the bombardment of thoughts going on in the area around the human heart. They were on to something that rings true to common experience.

From the list of examples just offered, one can see different forms of *logismoi* and the complexity involved in them. Some of the examples are temptations in the sense of suggestions to cease doing good or start doing something sinful. Others are more like rationalizations of sins or a setup for rationalization. Others are more accusatory, challenging the goodness or worth of the person or God. In real life, *logismoi* often come in webs of all such things woven together.

One reason for this is that *logismoi* can originate from different sources and condition each other. They can originate from the wounds of sin, bad habits, hurts and traumas of our lives, voices from our youth, memories of hurtful words, internalized shame, the customs and slogans of society, corrupt practices accepted in various institutions, the endless flow of imagery displayed on screens everywhere, biological factors, evil spirits or demons, and other sources. Traditionally, however, all the sources are traced back to three most general ones: the world, the flesh, and the devil.

Stepping back from particular examples of *logismoi* and their sources, we can study them in another way. The Fathers of the Church learned to classify the various *logismoi* and disordered passions that commonly afflict us. The ancient classifications come down to us today in the form of two major lists. In the Church of the West, there is the list of the seven deadly sins: gluttony, lust, greed, wrath, *acedia* (despondency), envy, and vanity.[30] In the Church of the East, there is the list of eight disordered passions: gluttony, lust, greed, wrath, melancholy, acedia, vanity, and pride. Each of these has many more specific forms and related offspring or symptoms: impurity, despair, cruelty, and many more. The lists are not simply a catechetical formula to be memorized. They are a perennially pertinent guide to recognizing the major symptoms and

---

30. The term *sloth* is a translation of the Latin term *acedia*, but the contemporary sense of the term *sloth* renders it a poor translation. *Acedia* is a much larger phenomenon, and sloth in the sense of laziness is but one related offspring or symptom. A better translation of *acedia* is despondency.

conditions of fallen human beings and the ordinary activities of demons. The lists shine a light on our inner life, help to protect it from evil, and promote its recovery. The lists tell us the most general forms of what Saint Paul calls the "thoughts of the flesh." The "thoughts of the flesh," he says, "are death" (Rom 8:6).[31]

A saying like "the thoughts of the flesh are death" might cause alarm in some people. People who suffer from severe insecurity, excessive anxiety, or deep-seated shame tend to find in every experience of *logismoi* a confirmation that something is terribly wrong with them. People who suffer from scrupulosity also tend to blow out of proportion the significance of *logismoi* in general. Scrupulosity tends to consider every one of them a sin, and to do so causes a great deal of false guilt and false shame. Interpretations and evaluations of *logismoi* born from severe insecurity, undue anxiety, deep-seated shame, and scrupulosity are an inaccurate guide to understanding the experience of *logismoi*, the truth about ourselves, or the truth about how God sees us. For there are important distinctions between the area around the heart and the deep heart, between what happens to us and what we do, between voluntary thoughts and involuntary ones, and the distinctions are morally important when it comes to the whole spectrum of our thoughts and passions in general. Learning these distinctions is both illuminating and essential for recovering from the pathos of the heart and receiving the renewal of our hearts by grace.

---

31. Translation by author.

The Renewal of the Heart

When Saint Paul says "the thoughts of the flesh are death," he does not mean that simply having *logismoi* or disordered passions is spiritual death. Under the influence of the world, the flesh, and the devil, we all suffer from *logismoi* appearing in the area around the heart. Depending on different people's overall condition, the bombardment upon the heart is more or less relentless. Yet it is one thing for *logismoi* to happen to us, and another thing for *logismoi* to be something we consent to or act on from our deep heart. What simply happens to us is involuntary. What we do is another thing: it is voluntary. *Logismoi* happen to us at first in the area around the heart, but they can only gain entrance to the deep heart if you or I freely consent to them or accept them. When Saint Paul says the "thoughts of the flesh are death," he means that *to consent* to them is spiritual death. Prior to our free acceptance and consent, they are merely *first movements* according to the traditional terminology. A first movement is not something we do, but something that happens to us, such as the image of gold that pops into the monk's head and triggers desire. But once a first movement happens to you or me in the area around the heart, it falls to each of us take a stand toward it from our deep hearts one way or another. Accept or reject?

It is the stance we take from our deep heart, not the mere occurrence of *logismoi* in the area around our heart, that determines who we become. First movements in themselves are not yet a part of our personal identity. It is important to note the point well. Many people are confused about what their own dark thoughts say about themselves, and the confusion unnecessarily worsens the pathos of the heart. The demons, too, might work to confuse us still more. They want us to believe that our thoughts and passions define us, or make us who we are, but no first movement or even recurring pattern of first movements is ever really the answer to the identity question. Only through free acceptance or consent do we take *logismoi* into our deep hearts and internalize them—or drink the poison, so to speak. Only then do *logismoi* really become part of our deep heart and part of the story of our personal identity.

Saint Catherine of Siena, for example, was once subjected to a relentless bombardment of lustful thoughts of horrible and vile forms for days, but not once did she consent to any of them.[32] Since the thoughts were just first movements, things that happened to her in the area around her heart, they did not determine her identity. The thoughts were not who she was. Rather, it was the stance of her deep heart against them that determined who she was in the long run. In fact, her persevering opposition to the flood of *logismoi* changed her increasingly into the particularly faithful, pure, and valiant woman who she was.

Obviously, your story and mine will not necessarily go the same way as hers. We do not always refuse or oppose *logismoi* so well. "The spirit indeed is willing, but the flesh is weak" (Mk 14:38). So, for all of us, at one point or another, the story

---

32. Raymond of Capua, *The Life of Catherine*, trans. Conleth Kearns (Wilmington, DE: Michael Glazier; Dublin: Dominican Publications, 1980), 98–99.

must be one of repenting after having succumbed. Repentance, as mentioned in the last chapter, consists of sorrow for sins committed together with the firm purpose of living one's life differently with the help of God's grace. Repentance is an amazing thing precisely because it consists of going back over old determinations of ourselves, undoing who we chose to become and to be in the past through sin, and determining to rewrite our answer to the identity question according to God's call to holiness. Because of lapses into sin, the overall story of our lives might be different from Saint Catherine's valiant refusal, but through repentance each of us can still have a truly great story in the end.

We see this in the lives of other saints. Saint Mary Magdalene, for example, was haunted with seven devils (see Mk 16:9). One traditional interpretation of her condition is that the seven devils were the demons behind the seven deadly sins. In this interpretation, Mary Magdalene had accepted them all at one point or another in her life. The Lord Jesus, however, cast them all out (see Mk 16:9). She spent the rest of her life in a state of grateful repentance—so grateful, in fact, that she stood at the foot of the Lord's cross. The Lord, in turn, granted her to become one of the first witnesses to the resurrection. Indeed, because the risen Lord told her to tell his other disciples of his resurrection (see Jn 20:17), she is called "the apostle to the apostles." According to some ancient traditions in the Church, she later traveled by boat with Martha, Lazarus, and other companions to the shores of southern France, where she settled in a cave in the mountains of Sainte-Baume. There she "lived as a hermit, praying, entrusting to the Lord all the people she met, all the people who came to meet her, all the people who came to seek refuge with her and asked her for help."[33]

After Saint Catherine had passed through her trial by many *logismoi* of lust, she asked the Lord where he was through it all. He answered: "in your heart."[34] The same holds true for all who have received the grace of Baptism and live in a state of grace. God dwells in our hearts, and he is ever at work in our hearts to renew his image and likeness in us. Renewal of the heart does not mean simply being restored to the state of the first human beings. The Garden of Eden is no more and never again shall it be. Rather, God has something better for us. When he pours the Spirit of Love into our hearts, the Spirit works to form in us not the first Adam but the last one—Jesus Christ himself. You and I know something the first humans never knew—the Holy Trinity—and our home now is not Eden but the Father's house in the heavenly places. And thanks to Jesus Christ, the gift of the Spirit, and the way of friendship in the Church, it is possible for us to go there. It is possible to receive a supernatural, mysterious, but real renewal of our hearts.

The Lord Jesus came into this world to break the shackles of *logismoi* and bring us up from drowning in automatic reactions to the world. He came to reorient the eyes of our hearts

---

33. "In Saint Baume," Le Sanctuaire de la Sainte-Baume, https//www.saintebaume.org/saint-mary-magdalene/. To this day, the Grotto of Saint Mary Magdalene stands in the mountains of southern France at the Sanctuaire de la Sainte-Baume. The Dominican Fathers have been the custodians of her relics in that place since 1295 and receive many pilgrims.

34. Raymond of Capua, *Life of Catherine*, 101.

to gazing Godward in contemplative prayer. He came to recuperate the first love of our hearts from fixating upon ourselves to burning with love for God. The Church prays for all of this in her liturgy. When we understand the pathos of the heart, and humbly admit our need for the healing of our hearts by grace, we can appreciate prayers of the Church all the more.

One prayer of the Mass goes like this: "O God, to whom every heart lies open, every desire speaks plainly, and from whom no secret is hidden, cleanse we pray the *thoughts* of our heart by the outpouring of the Holy Spirit. . . ."[35] Another says: "Pour your grace into our hearts, we pray, O Lord, that we may constantly be drawn away from *unruly desires*. . . ."[36] Finally, when lighting the paschal candle at the Easter Vigil, the priest says: "May the light of Christ rising in glory dispel the darkness of our hearts and minds."[37] In all of these ways and many more, the Church prays in the liturgy for your heart and mine to be delivered and healed of unruly thoughts and desires and for the image of God in us to be renewed by grace. Such is the hope of Christians in every generation, and "hope does not disappoint" (Rom 5:5).

35. "Opening Collect, Votive Mass of the Holy Spirit (B)," in the *Roman Missal*, 3rd typical ed. (Totowa, New Jersey: Catholic Book Publishing, 2021), 1186.

36. "Opening Collect, Friday of the Third Week of Lent," in the *Roman Missal*, 3rd typical ed., 104.

37. "Vigil in the Night," in the *Roman Missal*, 3rd typical ed., 200.

CHAPTER FIVE

The Practicals of the Way

A LL OF THE teachings and practices of the Church are given to the world in order to heal the pathos of the heart and transform us into Jesus by grace. Friendship with him is the way. Through faith and hope in his gracious love for us, and our love for him, the human heart gradually recovers from the pathological condition of the fall. Slowly do the eyes of the heart recover their spiritual sight. Slowly does the heart's first love reorient upon the Father of lights (see Jas 1:17). Slowly do we become the person God created us to be in the *communio* of the Church. The question now is about the practicals of the way of friendship. What must you and I do to walk this path?

A True Story of Transformation

Years ago, I had the joy of serving for several summers as a chaplain for Catholic college students involved in a summer formation program in the Rocky Mountains. Many of them had only recently returned to the practice of the faith. Like the prodigal son coming home, many had come from a long way off, and their hearts displayed the wounds of where they had wandered. They were looking for the answers to the three questions in their own lives, and the program gathered them in one place not only to learn the answers in theory but to live them out in practice. They committed their whole summer to living a seriously Catholic form of life together. In addition to working their daily jobs, they attended daily Mass, spent several hours each week in Eucharistic adoration, went to confession more often than usual, prayed the Rosary regularly (many of them did so daily), and participated in Bible studies, discipleship meetings, and theological talks. They regularly met with priests for conversation, attended weekend retreats, and spent significant time in silence and personal prayer each day. They formed holy friendships (a "dating fast" was in effect) and spent the summer living the *communio* of the Church in the breathtaking beauty of the Rockies. It was the actual practice of the way of friendship with God. Now, is it not obvious that such a way of life would transform someone?

It certainly did with these students. Only a few weeks into the summer, on one of the retreats, I gave them a conference on the pathos of the heart. It told the same story as the previous chapter of this book, and I explained how grace transforms us through the many practices of our faith. They all recognized themselves in the story and wondered why no one had explained this to them sooner. At this point in the summer, however, they had been living a seriously Catholic form of life for several weeks. They were taking part in all of the practices of the Catholic life, but in a more serious way. So, I asked them a question: Has all of this changed the manner in which you experience your own inner life? Virtually all of them said yes. And it was only a few weeks into the program. By the end of the summer, the testimonies to real transformation were over the top. Years later, it is still common to hear former participants say their lives have never been the same.

On the basis of experience with many other people, I could tell many more stories of lives changed on the way of friendship with God in the Church, but the point now is to consider a few essential practices time-tested and proven over the centuries. It is easy enough to list the important *exterior* practices: going to Mass at least every Sunday, going to confession, spending time in service and works of mercy, spending time in silence and meditation, spending time in Eucharistic adoration, praying the Rosary, prayerfully reading the Scriptures, studying the faith, reading the lives of the saints, seeking their intercession for specific graces, and seeking out the counsel of pastors to guide us. All of them, when practiced in different combinations and degrees suitable for different people, work together to heal us from the pathos of the heart. Through such ordinary practices, the grace of God given to us in Baptism actually grows within us, purifies and illuminates our hearts, and renews the image of God in us more and more. In ways known only to God, "Christ in you" grows more and more to the fullness of stature. In order for his grace to grow in us, however, it is also essential to learn something of the *interior* practices essential to living in union with him.

The Law of Love

The interior life is vast and rich. When it comes to practicals to guide the interior life, one will find innumerable instructions and counsels in the life of the Church. In order to get to the most essential thing quickly, the first thing to note is that in the spiritual life everything is about God. Or it should be. In all things, God is the proper focal point. All the many counsels and instructions out there on the spiritual life have no purpose except to refocus the eyes of the heart on God so that he might be our first love. The Lord Jesus is the Teacher, and he said, "If your eye is simple, your whole body will be filled with light" (see Mt 6:22). What he meant is that if you seek him first and above all, give him your heart's loving attention as continuously as possible, and cling to him in trust and love, then you will turn into him more and more—for he is the Light. But "if your eye is evil," i.e. if your deep heart is consenting to *logismoi* and given to serious sin, then "how great will the darkness be" (Mt 6:23 NABRE).

How, then, shall you and I live in order to keep our eyes fixed on Jesus (see Heb 12:2)? What must you and I do to walk in his Spirit of Love? Fortunately, someone already put this question to the Teacher, and he answered plainly: "'Hear, O Israel: The Lord our God, the Lord is one; and you shall love the Lord your God with all your heart, and with all your soul, and with all your mind, and with all your strength.' The second is this, 'You shall love your neighbor as yourself'" (Mk 12:29-30). The Lord's answer is traditionally called the greatest commandment or the law of love, and it tells us the essence of the way of friendship. The law of love is the primary rule of the heart. To call it a rule, law, or commandment is not to say it is merely an external norm or a demand imposed on us. Rather, the law of love is a *light* that educates us in the deepest longings of our own hearts—longings that flow from the grace of the Holy Spirit living and working within us.

In the midst of life, we need such a single rule or light of the heart. A single rule cuts through what is sometimes a bewildering variety of spiritual instructions, gives clarity to the mind, and steadies the ship on one course. Throughout any given day, our attention and intentions tend to scatter in many directions. A single memorable rule is like an inner pathway of return to the heart—to the one thing necessary. The law of love leads to the real center of our lives: union with God.

Hear, O Israel . . .

The first part of the rule says: *Hear, O Israel, the Lord our God, the Lord is one.* Let us note the first word. *Hear*, it says. For "faith comes from what is heard" (Rom 10:17), and "faith," according to Saint Thomas Aquinas, "is the foundation of the entire spiritual edifice."[38] God reveals himself and many mysteries to us, and faith takes his word for all of it. Scripture and tradition contain innumerable mysteries of faith—the articles of the Creed, the mysteries of the Rosary, and much more—and the Church sets them before us in

---

38. Saint Thomas Aquinas, *Commentary on the Sentences*, d. 23, q. 2, q.1, a.1, ad 1.

various ways for us to take them on the Word of God. Faith is
a free and simple assent to all of it because God has revealed it
all. Faith is a precious gift and the key to growth in union with
God. Our first call, therefore, is to listen to God speak his
mysteries, and to believe in God and his Word.

O Israel, it says. God is addressing us in these words, and
by addressing us calls us to live *cor ad cor* or heart-to-heart
with him in a life of prayer and relationship. He calls us by the
name of *Israel*. According to one ancient etymology of the
word, common among the rabbis as well as the Fathers of the
Church, *Israel* means "mind beholding God."[39] When the
Lord calls us Israel, he reveals how he is calling us to become
contemplative souls. For contemplative souls tend to become
Jesus Christ by the power of the Spirit in the depths of their
hearts. "And we all, with unveiled face, beholding the glory of
the Lord, are being changed into his likeness from one degree
of glory to another; for this comes from the Lord who is the
Spirit" (2 Cor 3:18).

Contemplative souls are not just priests, monks, nuns, or
active religious. A contemplative soul is someone given to
listening to God, looking for God, pondering God and his
mysteries in the depths of the heart. To be given to such
things is not reserved to priests and religious: *all* the baptized are called to contemplative prayer. Contemplative

---

39. James H. Charlesworth, *The Old Testament Pseudepigrapha* (London:
Darton, Longman & Todd, 1983–85), 703. For only one example of the
Fathers using this etymology, see Pseudo-Macarius, *Fifty Spiritual Homilies
and The Great Letter*, trans. George Maloney, S.J. (New York: Paulist Press,
1992), 234: "Israel is interpreted as being the mind contemplating God."

prayer simply means "a gaze of faith fixed on Jesus, an attentiveness to the Word of God, a silent love" (CCC 2724). Contemplative prayer, when it grows strong in our hearts, is real personal familiarity with God. It is intimacy with God in the deepest sense. Intimacy with God is awareness of and amazement at his Presence living in us and acting all around us in many ways. By calling us *Israel,* God is inviting us—one and all—to walk the path that leads to such a loving awareness of his Presence, that is, to contemplative prayer. More on contemplative prayer in chapters to come.

For now, the first step and practical takeaway is simple: *believe in his Love.* The essential practice of the heart is always first to believe in God and his mysteries—especially in his Love. For believing in his Love is how we drink in his Spirit of Love and grow to walk as Jesus Christ walked. According to Saint John of the Cross, faith is what really establishes someone in union with God.[40] Imagination *per se* does not do so, rational analysis *per se* does not do so, even private revelations *per se* do not do so. Faith does so. More specifically, it is "faith working through love" (Gal 5:6). When it is love that inspires our faith, our loving faith is like the hemorrhaging woman in Mark's Gospel (see Mk 5:25–34). Just as she reached out and touched the hem of the Lord's garment, and power went forth from him to heal her, so our loving faith in the Lord Jesus spiritually touches the hem of his garment in heaven. When our hearts touch him spiritually with a loving

---

40. Karol Wojtyla, *Faith According to St. John of the Cross*, trans. Jordan Aumann (San Francisco: Ignatius Press, 1981), 33.

faith, power flashes from him in the heavenly places and passes into our souls. New graces are given—a new breath of his Spirit. To touch the risen Lord Jesus through loving faith is the essential interior practice for living in union with him, clinging to him in love, and so being turned into him more and more in the depths of our souls.

Loving faith is like a ray of divine light illuminating the eyes of the heart. It is the beginning and wellspring of contemplative prayer. What energizes loving faith most of all is to consider how much "he first loved us" (1 Jn 4:19). Remember the cross of Jesus Christ. Remember how he knew us and loved us, each one and all, from the cross (CCC 478). And "remember Jesus Christ, risen from the dead" (2 Tim 2:8). Let us never surrender the memory of the Lord and his love. "Abide in my love," says the Lord (Jn 15:9). What does that mean in practical terms? "Believe in his love for you," said Saint Elizabeth of the Trinity, "in his exceeding Love."[41]

The Love of God

The second part of the rule says: *You shall love the Lord your God with all your heart, and with all your soul, and with all your mind, and with all your strength.* Saint Thomas Aquinas interprets it as follows.[42] Heart, in this context, signifies something in the deep heart, namely, the will. More specifically, it signifies one's first love and first intention. To

---

41. *The Complete Works of Elizabeth of the Trinity*, 128.
42. *Summa Theologiae* II–II, q. 45, a. 4 and a. 5.

love God with all your heart is to seek God above all. A God-seeking heart organizes everything in life around him, and directs us from within to live for God—to go to God—in and through all that we do or suffer. Soul, in this context, signifies the images and passions in the whole area around the heart. To love God with your whole soul is to withhold consent from *logismoi* and disordered passions, and strive to coordinate the whole spectrum of thoughts and passions according to the truth. For love "does not rejoice in wrong-doing, but rejoices in the truth" (1 Cor 13:6 NRSV). Mind, in this context, stands for eyes of the heart (also called intellect). To love God with your whole mind is to submit your intellect to God through faith, to listen to him, to gaze upon him with affection, and to evaluate and judge all things in his light. Finally, strength signifies external actions. Our bodies and outward behaviors are also an essential part of being human. To love God with all your strength is to comport yourself properly as a human being, as a member of the Mystical Body of Christ, and as a participant in the *communio* of his Church. The moral teachings of the Church tell us what proper comportment is in practice. God gives his moral teachings to us for our good, for the good of the whole human race, and for his glory.

The sacrament of Baptism ignites in each of us the flame of such a wholehearted love for God. The flame of love is meant to grow, and our calling is to protect and promote it until our hearts become a burning furnace of charity. The way to protect and promote it—the practical takeaway—is to *watch at all times and pray*. Watchfulness or vigilance is no small theme in Scripture. The Lord said to his disciples,

"*Watch at all times*, praying that you may have strength to escape all these things that will take place and to stand before the Son of man" (Lk 21:36). The "things that will take place," in the literal sense, are the events to come at the end of the world. But, in a spiritual sense, this means the approach of the *logismoi* that will come today. Saint Paul says clearly, "*Pray at all times in the Spirit. To that end keep alert . . .*" (Eph 6:18, emphasis added).

Watchfulness, wakefulness, and prayerfulness are not marginal or transitory matters in the spiritual life.[43] Rather, each of them must be ongoing, steadfast, and persistent. They are essential for protecting and promoting a loving faith and a wholehearted love of God. The ancient monks had much to say about watchfulness or vigilance and found great spiritual help in the practice of it. Their lessons are timely for us today. So, how did they understand it?

In the deep heart, each of us stands at once before God and the whole area around the heart. Watchfulness or vigilance has two senses. In the first sense, it is the habit of guarding the deep heart from consent to *logismoi* and disordered passions. Just as a soldier guarding a fort scans the horizon and refuses entrance to approaching strangers, so the watchful person scans the area around his or her heart and refuses entrance to approaching *logismoi* and disordered passions. Vigilance, in this sense, calls for a certain *awareness* of what is

---

43. The presentation of vigilance here, especially understanding of it in terms of awareness, resistance, and eradication of *logismoi*, is based upon *Christ Our Pascha: Catechism of the Ukrainian Greek Catholic Church*, nos. 752–754, 796–7988.

actually going on in our hearts. Such awareness grows over the course of our spiritual development. The more prayerful one becomes, the more sensitive one becomes to what is approaching.

Vigilance also calls for *resistance* of the deep heart to *logismoi* upon first notice of their approach. Though we cannot control what comes to us in the area around the heart, with the help of grace it is possible for us to withhold consent to *logismoi* from the depths of our hearts. Few of us, however, can hold out for long—especially against more disturbing *logismoi*. So, true vigilance also means asking God for help and mercy all the time, but especially at the first approach of *logismoi*. "Watch at all times, *praying . . .*" says the Lord (Lk 21:36, emphasis added). To watch at all times and pray is one of the most important ways to walk in friendship with the Lord. It can be challenging. Sentries on watch tend to become sleepy, and so do we when it comes to guarding the heart. In the Garden of Gethsemane, the disciples fell asleep, and the Lord shook them awake: "Could you not watch with me one hour?" (Mt 26:40). It was a call to vigilance.

In a second sense, vigilance is the habit of the deep heart looking out not for sin, but for God. It is a wakefulness, an alertness, an interior orientation to eternity. The lack of vigilance in this sense, the lack of interior orientation to eternity, is one of the sources—hidden in the depths of people's hearts—of the secularization our world is now undergoing. The Fathers of the Church sometimes called the lack of interior orientation to eternity the *forgetfulness of God*. The forgetfulness of God is a tendency not to seek God, nor to consider God much or at crucial junctures. It can even harden into a deep oblivion to God. Some of the Fathers thought that the forgetfulness of God was at the root of the first sin of the first human beings. To be watchful for God, to stay awake on the lookout for him, not only lays the axe to the root of sin and secularization, but also positively promotes the loving faith that brings us into deeper union with God. Vigilance means remembering God—living in his Presence.

Vigilance in the sense of guarding the deep heart is for the sake of vigilance in the sense of looking to eternity. Vigilance means being on the lookout against approaching *logismoi* in order to be on the lookout for God—always believing in his Love. The monks of old learned by experience that the steadfast practice of the twofold vigilance works wonders of inner freedom over the long haul. A steadfast vigilance tends to turn into a life of ongoing prayer. It turns into consistently *relating* to Jesus Christ, really living life together with the Lord from one moment to the next. One learns to speak honestly with God even about all the *logismoi* one is enduring and to ask humbly for his help and healing.

The eradication of the roots of the *logismoi* in our life is a long-term process. It is a work of divine grace purifying the heart, yet watchfulness and prayerfulness are essential for receiving such graces in a really fruitful way—essential for the heart to be healed of its pathos, for the image of God to be renewed by grace, and for each of us to become like Jesus. Watchfulness and prayerfulness lead a person, gradually and by stages, to "the peace of God that surpasses all understanding" (Phil 4:7 NABRE). They lead to "a gentle and quiet spirit" (1 Pet 3:4): the awareness of Christ himself living in our heart, the awareness of the indwelling Spirit (see 1 Cor

3:16), and the awareness of the Father (see Jn 14:23). "You will never be commonplace," said Saint Elizabeth of the Trinity, "if you are vigilant in love."[44]

The Love of Neighbor

The third part of the rule says: *You shall love your neighbor as yourself.* The Lord also says, "Love one another as I have loved you" (Jn 15:12). To love oneself properly, to love one's neighbor as oneself, and to love as Jesus loves are challenging matters indeed, and it takes a lifetime of grace and truth to learn what it really means to love in all three ways. One of the most comprehensive Scripture studies of charity ever composed is by the scholar Ceslas Spicq.[45] After studying every instance of the term charity (*agape*) in the New Testament, and in many texts beyond it, he concluded that, according to Scripture, charity is a form of love not of this world. It is primarily an attribute of God. It is God's love poured into our hearts through the Holy Spirit. When he comes to dwell in our hearts through Baptism, the Spirit in turn forms our hearts to love all people with a certain reverence or respect for each particular human person.

Two things distinguish such love from all other forms of love. It is not based on any bond of nature, such as family or

---

44. *The Complete Works of Elizabeth of the Trinity*, 180.

45. Ceslas Spicq, O.P., *Agape in the New Testament*, trans. Sister Marie Aquinas McNamara and Sister Mary Honoria Richter, 3 vols. (St. Louis: B. Herder Bool, 1963–66). For a condensed version of his account of charity, see Ceslas Spicq, O.P., *Charity and Liberty in the New Testament* (Staten Island, New York: Alba House, 1965).

citizenship, or on any personal preference for people, such as natural friendships. Charity is for all human beings. Yet charity is concerned first and foremost with the one who is nearest to us—the neighbor. The Parable of the Good Samaritan drives both points home in a simple but compelling story (see Lk 10:25–37). The Samaritan is intent on helping the particular victim whom he happens across on the road. His love is not based on tribal or ethnic fellowship, but on concern for the person who is nearest to him in that moment.

Is it possible to love all people with such a personal reverence and respect? All of us are subject to certain physical limits as to how many people we can know, love, and serve. According to the teaching of Saint Thomas Aquinas, charity brings with it a certain good-will, mercy, and beneficence toward all people, even sinners, but in practice charity loves those people who are in fact known and nearest to us according to a certain order of proximity.[46] First comes proper love of oneself in the sense of avoiding all sin. Second comes love of family members, for it is wrong to neglect them in the name of the love of strangers. Third comes love of those farther removed from us, but still near to us in various ways. The same principle applies to the Church as a sort of family of ours. You and I are called to love one another who are *in* the Church even though it can often be quite challenging to do so. The practical takeaway comes to this: "Do good to all, but especially those who are of the household of faith" (Gal 6:10).[47]

---

46. *Summa Theologiae* III, qs. 25 & 26, 30 & 31.

47. Translation by author.

In order for us to be transformed into Jesus Christ by the power of the Holy Spirit, the Teacher has taught us the way of friendship and given us a single rule of the heart. *Hear O Israel . . . you shall love the Lord your God . . . and your neighbor as yourself.* Let us keep the law of love ever in our sight—believing in his Love, watchful and prayerful at all times, always doing good to all people as much as we can with the help of divine grace. The law of love and the takeaways we have discussed in this chapter ground us and guide us on the way of friendship. They are the first and foremost practicals of the way, because on the way of friendship love energizes and inspires everything. However, there are many further practicals of the way—many more lessons to learn and steps to take on the road to deeper union and identification with Jesus. All of them, as we will see in the next chapter, are summed up in the Beatitudes.

CHAPTER SIX

The Beatitudes

T HE HOLY SPIRIT is an iconographer who engraves the image of Jesus Christ into our hearts. The process calls for you and me to live as Jesus lived. If anyone should ask precisely *how* or *in what specific ways* you and I should do so, the answer is in the Beatitudes. For "the Beatitudes depict the countenance of Christ and portray his charity" (CCC 1717). Jesus Christ is the one who lived the Beatitudes first and to the full, and as *his* acts they are like rays of light shining from his heart. The grace to practice the Beatitudes flows from the heart of Jesus into our own, and practicing each of them in turn likens our hearts to his.

The Beatitudes are teachings of the Lord so deep, so profound, and so rich in eternal wisdom that all the commentaries of the ages have yet to get to the bottom of them. One might study them from a thousand different angles and find marvels from every point of view. They speak to everyone at every point on the journey. They contain mystical medicines for the pathos of the heart and light up the pathway to the Father's House. The order of the Beatitudes is well worth noting. For they form a sequence of lessons to learn and steps to take in following Jesus Christ.[48] The Beatitudes are a true *formation program* for personal union and identification with the eternal Son of God. The Virgin Mary lived the Beatitudes eminently and perfectly, and the saints lived them to a very high degree. The Virgin and the saints together help us by their prayers to live the Beatitudes as well. For all of heaven knows that whosoever shall practice the Beatitudes will surely become another Christ in this world by the power of the Holy Spirit.

To walk the road of the Beatitudes, however, you and I must do three things. The first is to *ponder* how the Lord Jesus lived each of them. The second is to *pray* for the grace to do the same. The third is to *practice* each one to the fullest extent possible given where we actually are today. An honest

---

48. Saint Augustine, *Commentary on the Lord's Sermon on the Mount*, trans. Denis J. Kavanagh, O.S.A. (New York: Fathers of the Church, 1951). According to Saint Augustine, the Sermon on the Mount summarizes the whole teaching of Jesus Christ, and the Beatitudes more specifically are a complete list of the essential lessons to learn, steps to take, and stages to pass through on the way to union and identification with Jesus Christ. For Augustine, in addition to the law of love, the Beatitudes chart the whole course you and I must walk as disciples of Jesus Christ in order to become like him. For more on the sequence of the Beatitudes, see the sources cited in fn. 47.

acknowledgment of our weaknesses, our limitations, and our radical need for God is, in fact, the very place to begin.[49]

Blessed are the poor in spirit . . .

Blessed are the poor in spirit, for theirs is the kingdom of heaven. To be poor in spirit is to be aware of just how much one needs God, yet completely confident that he will take care of everything. The poor in spirit know and humbly accept their own weaknesses, limitations, and fragilities. Despite whatever excellences they might have of the natural order, and despite whatever standing they might have before others, insofar as they stand before God in their hearts they are nothing but little ones. Their hearts are focused on looking to the Father, counting on him for love and grace—especially when pain and afflictions mount up. Jesus demonstrated such

---

49. The following meditations on the Beatitudes are based on Augustine's *Commentary on the Lord's Sermon on the Mount*; Saint Thomas Aquinas, *Summa Theologiae* I–II q. 69; Saint Thomas Aquinas, *Catena Aurea*, trans. John Henry Newman. vol. 1 (London: Saint Austin Press, 1997), 145–160; Saint Gregory of Nyssa, *The Lord's Prayer & The Beatitudes*, trans. Hilda C. Graef. (London: Longman's, Green, 1954); Ambrose Gardeil, O.P., *The Holy Spirit in the Christian Life* (St. Louis: Herder, 1954); Servais Pinckaers, O.P., *The Sources of Christian Ethics*, trans. Sr. Mary Thomas Noble, O.P. (Washington, DC: The Catholic University of America Press, 1995), ch. 6; Servais Pinckaers, O.P., *Happiness God's Way: Living the Beatitudes*, trans. Sister Mary Thomas Noble, O.P. (Alba House, 1998); Jacques Philippe, *The Way of Trust and Love: A Retreat Guided by St. Therese of Lisieux*, trans. Helena Scott (New York, Scepter: 2012); Jacques Philippe, *The Eight Doors of the Kingdom* (New York: Scepter, 2018).

a heart throughout his life, but especially in his whole agony, passion, and death. He accepted weakness on the cross (see 2 Cor 13:4), and through it all he looked to the Father. In his last breath, he revealed the deepest lifelong intention of his heart: "Father, into your hands I commend my spirit" (Lk 23:46 NABRE).

In our own time, Saint Thérèse of Lisieux has brought to light once again for the Church how poverty of spirit is the place to remain before God. It is a healthy and holy self-acceptance, and a handing of oneself over to God in confidence and trust. She calls it the Little Way. The essence of the Little Way is love, or friendship with God, but humility and confidence are the necessary conditions of the heart for love to unfold. Egocentrism, vanity, pride, self-reliance, the desire to control everything, and the tendency to interpret everything as if it were "all about me" seriously impede love. They are also a set-up for disappointment, discouragement, and despair in the spiritual life. Poverty of spirit, humility, and littleness, on the other hand, oppose the *logismoi* of pride and vanity before the heart consents to them. According to Saint John Climacus, in fact, humility is the destroyer of *all* disordered passions.[50] Poverty of spirit lays the axe to the root.

Blessed are those who mourn . . .

Blessed are those who mourn, for they shall be comforted. To mourn, in the context of this Beatitude, is to suffer the loss of

---

50. Saint John Climacus, *The Ladder of Divine Ascent* (Boston: Holy Transfiguration Monastery, 2019), 180.

various things for the sake of the kingdom. It can refer to the loss of good things or bad things, but in its most basic sense it means sorrow or contrition over sins committed. The first step in practicing this Beatitude is a trip to the sacrament of Penance. To go to the sacrament of Penance can be a sorrowful experience, but it leads to a happy liberation from the guilt of sin. True contrition for sin includes the intention to walk away from sinful things and to live differently. Walking away and living differently, however, ordinarily require a tearful break with "the sweets of folly."[51] The sweets of folly are a variety of *logismoi*, and the second Beatitude serves to remedy them. *Gluttony*, for example, is the disordered desire for food and drink, *lust* for sexual pleasure, and *greed* for riches, wealth, or external goods. Such disordered passions, once freely accepted, tend to introduce still further disorders, such as melancholy and acedia. *Melancholy* is a disordered sadness over the loss of good things, and *acedia* is a disordered sadness about spiritual goods or aversion to spiritual practices. Those who freely consent to such sinful or immoderate passions tend to form an attachment to the sweets of folly. Repentance is sorrowful *because* of the passionate attachment to them, yet repentance is the only path to freedom.

The Lord promises the comfort of the Spirit to those who accept the rule of moderation and seek to break the chains that enslave. His comfort often comes in the form of a new inner freedom from domination by impulses, greater self-possession, and inner peace. Charity blazing in the heart has a

---

51. Saint Augustine, *Confessions*, IX.i.1, 155.

joy all its own. The tearful break with the sweets of folly works wonders for the soul.

Yet the Spirit sometimes calls us to break not only with sin, but even with certain reasonable and legitimate goods. One example is fasting. To eat and drink in moderation is a good thing, but certain days and seasons are appointed for fasting. Jesus fasted in the desert for forty days to set an example for us (see Mt 4:1–2). It is good for the soul in many ways and is a chance to sacrifice for sinners in imitation of the Lord. Recent popes have urged the revival of fasting even outside the season of Lent.[52] There are other examples besides fasting. Private property, marriage, and one's personal freedom are all good things, but the Spirit calls many people to walk away from them and make vows of poverty, celibate chastity, and obedience. No one can follow the evangelical counsels without enduring a moment of sorrow for the loss, yet the Lord promises a hundredfold to those who do so (see Mk 10:29–31).

Our lives in this world will also inevitably include the loss of many good things such as health, friends, and family. Everyone mourns in one way or another. When our sufferings are brought into the friendship with the Lord, accepted in

---

52. Pope Saint Paul VI, *Paenitimini*; Pope Saint John Paul II in multiple forms: General Audience, March 21, 1979 (https://www.vatican.va/content/john-paul-ii/en/audiences/1979/documents/hf_jp-ii_aud_19790321.html) & Angelus, March 10, 1996 (https://www.vatican.va/content/john-paul-ii/it/angelus/1996/documents/hf_jp-ii_ang_19960310.html); Pope Benedict XVI, Message for Lent, 2009 (https://www.vatican.va/content/benedict-xvi/en/messages/lent/documents/hf_ben-xvi_mes_20081211_lent-2009.html).

mystery, and offered up for the conversion of sinners, the Spirit is there to comfort us and draw us into a real union of hearts with the Lord. For the Lord Jesus mourned on the cross as no human being ever did. He did not mourn for his own sins but for ours, and he did penance for us all out of love. He broke with all the goods of nature on the cross, and in so doing he mourned. Yet he received it all back in the resurrection with the most indescribable comfort of a glorified body.

Saint John the Baptist went into the desert to fast and pray, and his example is a permanent lesson in how to repent, break with sin, watch at all times, and pray in the Spirit. Obviously, the Spirit does not call everyone to the same measure of asceticism as John the Baptist, but everyone can and should pray for the grace of a healthy and holy self-denial. Everyone should take the steps needed to find the balance suitable for oneself. We often need the advice of competent guides about particular issues, but speaking generally, the right balance is the one that best protects and promotes fullness of life according to one's overall vocation at present—especially the life of love and prayer in the depths of the heart.

Blessed are the meek . . .

Blessed are the meek, for they shall inherit the earth. Meekness is the proper way to deal with passions such as anger, animosity, resentment, and bitterness. What provokes such passions is always a sense of injury or injustice either to oneself or to others. The injury might be real or merely perceived, but when we sense an injury or injustice of any kind, our passions naturally move toward vengeance. The tendency is to return evil for evil, but meekness regulates and seriously subdues such passions. Meekness is not simply unresistance to evil, but resistance to evil with a certain gentle but firm spirit of opposition. Meekness is how *love* opposes injury and injustice.

Jesus demonstrated great meekness in his passion. He showed firmness when he set his face like flint for Jerusalem (see Is 50:7; Lk 9:51), but gentleness when he turned the other cheek to those who struck his face. Yes, he was like a Lamb led to the slaughter (see Is 53:7), but he also opposed certain injuries with measured words: "If I have spoken wrongly, testify to the wrong: but if I have spoken rightly, why do you strike me?" (Jn 18:23 NABRE). Perfect meekness consists in not returning "evil for evil, or insult for insult; but, on the contrary, a blessing" (1 Pet 3:9 NABRE; see Rom 12:17). Jesus displayed such perfect meekness when, in the midst of crucifixion, he prayed for his executioners: "Father, forgive them; for they know not what they do" (Lk 23:34).

How to remedy immoderate anger is one of the great questions of the spiritual life. One essential remedy for excessive anger and lingering resentments is forgiveness. The topic of forgiveness deserves a special discussion all its own, especially for those who have been gravely injured by others.[53] But one of the most important ways for all of us to grow in meekness is to learn to look at every human being in a certain specific light—as made in the image of God, beloved of God, and

---

53. For a brief, powerful, and practical guide to forgiveness, see Robert DeGrandis, S.S.J., *To Forgive is Divine* (DeGrandis Publishing, 1981).

precious in his sight. We must all ask for the grace to see people for who they are according to God, and that often means looking at them with new eyes. Doing so serves to form a higher understanding of others, especially those who disturb us, and expands our ability to respond to them without animosity. With meekness goes a spirit of gentleness and kindness.

One saint who learned meekness was Saint Elizabeth of the Trinity. As a young girl, she was prone to particularly extreme tantrums—so much so that the neighbors remarked on them frequently to her mother. She tended to perceive injury where there was none or to overreact where an injury was slight. As Elizabeth grew, her tantrums turned into increasingly serious confrontations with her mother. At one point, her mother had even packed Elizabeth's bags by the door and threatened to send her to the local reform house for girls who had been rescued from living on the streets. It was all to no avail. At the same time, however, Elizabeth also had a great love for prayer and holy things. One day, when she was preparing to receive her First Holy Communion at the age of nine, Elizabeth went through a particularly bad moment of anger. Her mother shrewdly resorted to the threat of postponing Elizabeth's First Holy Communion for a year. Faced with the choice between indulging her anger and gaining something she loved more, Elizabeth finally resolved to temper her anger voluntarily. It would take no small number of years, praying for the grace of patience, and efforts to keep her deep heart from consenting to first movements of anger, but Elizabeth eventually became known as a remarkably self-possessed, seriously composed, and socially graceful young

woman. In fact, she became known for her gentleness and
kindness toward all. The masters of prayer in every age tell us
that meekness is a necessary condition for growth in contemplative prayer. A soul full of anger cannot pray in stillness,
silence, and peace. Having learned meekness, Elizabeth her-
self went on to become one of the greatest masters of contemplative prayer of all time.[54]

Blessed are those who hunger and thirst for righteousness . . .

*Blessed are those who hunger and thirst for righteousness,
for they shall be satisfied.* Some translations say hunger and
thirst for *righteousness* and other translations say hunger and
thirst for *justice.* One emphasizes longing for a right relationship with God and the other emphasizes longing for right
relationships between human beings. The Lord is teaching us
to long for both—for his saving and ordering influence to permeate our own souls and set things right before him as well as
to permeate the whole order of human affairs and relationships and set all things right there too. The beatitude, therefore, touches on all the desires and hopes human beings carry
for a new heart and a new world.

When it comes to right relationship with God, the Fathers
of the Church interpret this beatitude in terms of longing to
hear and obey the divine Word or the divine Will. The Lord

---

54. See Joanne Mosley, *Elizabeth of the Trinity: The Unfolding of Her
Message,* vol. 1, *In the World & In Community* (Oxford: Teresian Press,
2012), chs. 1 and 2.

spoke of his own hunger and thirst for righteousness in this sense. He revealed his deepest hunger when he said, "My food is to do the will of him who sent me" (Jn 4:34). He also revealed what cup he preferred: "My Father, if it be possible, let this cup pass from me; nevertheless, not as I will, but as thou wilt" (Mt 26:39). To hunger and thirst for God's righteousness means one seeks to please God above all—even more than one seeks to please oneself—and the Lord demonstrated such love for the Father on the cross. Under the influence of the pathos of the heart, however, we tend to love ourselves more than God. Real healing of the heart means coming to a place where we love God more than ourselves. After all, such is the mark of true friends. Friends just seek to please one another.

When it comes to knowing what pleases God, he has revealed it to us in Scripture and tradition. We can learn to recognize what pleases God through regular *lectio divina*—a prayerful way of reading Scripture. It is a practical way to listen to God. God speaks to us in the sacred page unlike anywhere else. Particular words often leap out, strike the heart, and show each of us personally the way to go. Even when no such thing happens, however, ongoing meditation on the words of Scripture throughout the day, as well as study of the faith overall, tends to form in us a broad understanding of what pleases God, a well-formed conscience, and a sort of Catholic common-sense. These things, in turn, can help us judge what pleases God here and now without a lot of undue introspection or anxiety. No one need obsess about the will of God. In time, a regular practice of *lectio divina* gradually purifies the heart, illumines the mind, and directs our actions in the way of peace.

When it comes to right relationship between people, the Fathers of the Church interpret this beatitude in terms of working for people to receive what is their due. The Lord Jesus came preaching good news to the poor, release to captives, and liberty for those who are oppressed (see Lk 4:16–19). The fallen heart cares much for such things when it comes to ourselves, but tends to care far less when it comes to other people—especially those who are not family or friends. Real healing of the heart means coming to a place where seeking justice for other people becomes a true intention and concern of our own heart too. From conditions of dire poverty, to human trafficking and abuse, to the victims of violence, torture, and war, there is no shortage of standing injustices in the world. Those who hunger and thirst for righteousness simply set about washing the feet, so to speak, of those who are beaten down, seeking to help in whatever little ways are possible.

Saint Teresa of Calcutta is an amazing example of someone who hungered and thirsted for righteousness in both senses. Because of her devotion to seeking a right relationship with God, she received a special inspiration to understand the Lord's words from the cross, "I thirst" (Jn 19:28), and consequently his will for her life. She vividly realized how the Lord thirsted for her love from the cross, and how he thirsted for her to love him in the poor and despised. So, she devoted her life completely to slaking his thirst in whatever disguise he might come to her—especially in the poorest of the poor. In her hunger and thirst for righteousness, she amazed the world with a compassion that was unafraid to touch some of the most broken and afflicted people on the earth. She is also an example of the next beatitude.

Blessed are the merciful . . .

Blessed are the merciful, for they shall obtain mercy. Mercy is love healing people's afflictions. There is no end to the number of hurting and suffering people in our world. To be merciful is to have a heart moved with compassion at the afflictions of others, and the tendency of compassion is to reach out to alleviate them. "My heart is moved with pity for the crowd," said the Lord (Mk 8:2 NABRE), so he "went about doing good and healing all that were oppressed by the devil" (Acts 10:38). The passion of the Lord is his ultimate work of mercy: "By his stripes we are healed" (see Is 53:5). The more you and I practice merciful love to those who are hurting and afflicted, the more our hearts grow to be like his—this is a real union and identification with the compassionate heart of Jesus Christ.

But how? The traditional list of corporal and spiritual works of mercy still stands.[55] Such deeds are essentially pleasing to God. The Lord lives his thirst for love in other people, especially in those who are hurting the most, and the littlest signs of charity have supernatural ramifications far beyond our perception. For "God loves a cheerful giver" (2 Cor 9:7). It matters little whether the works are great or small,

---

55. The seven corporal works of mercy are: 1. Feed the hungry, 2. Give drink to the thirsty, 3. Clothe the naked, 4. Visit the imprisoned, 5. Shelter the homeless, 6. Visit the sick, 7. Bury the dead. The seven spiritual works of mercy are: 1. Admonish the sinner, 2. Instruct the ignorant, 3. Counsel the doubtful, 4. Comfort the sorrowful, 5. Bear wrongs patiently, 6. Forgive all injuries, 7. Pray for the living and the dead. See CCC 2447.

organized projects or random acts in daily life. The measure of love for God and neighbor in each gesture is what matters the most. The risen Lord Jesus will remember every last one of them. "At the evening of life," Saint John of the Cross says, "we will be judged on love" (CCC 1022). So, let us ask for the grace to practice the works of mercy and set about like the Lord doing good for those nearest to us who are afflicted.

One example of mercy is the American woman Rose Hawthorne.[56] She was the daughter of the novelist Nathaniel Hawthorne, and she converted to Catholicism in 1891 at the age of forty. Within a few years, around 1894, she learned of the plight of cancer victims in New York. In her day, cancer was thought to be contagious. Those diagnosed with incurable cancer were sent home if their relatives could afford to care for them. If they were incurable and poor, however, they often lost their jobs and their homes, either because employers and landlords feared the disease or because their illness made them too sick to work and they could not pay their rent. They were left to find their own place to die, or they were sent to the notorious Blackwell's Island just off the Manhattan shore. There they were confined to atrocious "hospitals" or almshouses and left to die. Whether homeless in New York or condemned to Blackwell's, the result was the same: they ended their days without proper care or any comfort. Rose Hawthorne set out to give them a home in their last days and serve them in whatever little ways she could. After a brief course in nursing, it all began with bandaging the face of Mrs.

---

56. Her cause for canonization is now underway, and she is presently a Servant of God.

Mary Watson, who would later become her first guest in her tenement apartment on the Lower East Side. From that day on, Rose was dedicated to caring for those dying with cancer, especially those who were poor and had no one to help them. Soon, other women joined her special work of mercy, and eventually they became the Dominican Sisters of Hawthorne. To this day, her Sisters run homes for anyone diagnosed with terminal cancer but too poor to afford care at the end of life. The Sisters mercifully care for each person to the end.

Blessed are the pure in heart . . .

Blessed are the pure in heart, for they shall see God. Purity of heart is an interior quality with two sides. On the one hand, a pure heart lacks any voluntary consent to *logismoi* or to first movements toward sin. Even if bombarded by *logismoi* in the area around the heart, someone remains pure in this sense so long as he or she does not voluntarily yield. Human beings are always susceptible to at least *some* outbreaks of disorderly thoughts and passions, but when our hearts are purified through healing and renewal, the deep heart will consent to them less and less over time, and even the unruly outbreaks tend to diminish. Our fallen hearts are a bit like mixed metal—for example, silver mixed with lead. They have the good tendencies and inclinations of our nature, but problematic tendencies and bad habits too. The Lord is like a refiner (see Mal 3:3). His graces of purification—achieved by following the law of love and practicing the Beatitudes—separate the silver from the lead in our hearts. Through such means, we receive the grace of greater purity of heart.

On the other hand, purity of heart is the fullness of charity or love. One of the desert Fathers, Abba Moses, said that the pure heart has all the elements of love enumerated in 1 Corinthians 13.[57] "Love is patient and kind, love is not jealous or boastful; it is not arrogant or rude. Love does not insist on its own way; it is not irritable or resentful; it does not rejoice at wrong, but rejoices in the right. Love bears all things, believes all things, hopes all things, endures all things" (1 Cor 13:4–7). A heart on fire with such charity is a pure heart indeed, and the only question is just how brightly the furnace of the heart shall come to blaze.

As the beatitude promises, the masters of prayer in every age have found that purity of heart leads to contemplative prayer. Contemplative prayer is something like seeing God but in a manner different from heaven. It is a simple gaze of faith fixed on Jesus. The grace of contemplative prayer is like a ray of heavenly light that "illumines the eyes of our heart and teaches us to see everything in the light of his truth and his compassion for all men" (CCC 2715). Under the influence of the Spirit of wisdom, contemplative souls can "taste and see that the Lord is good" (Ps 34:8). Such contemplative prayer is more common than people might realize, and Christians commonly experience flashes of it here or there. All the baptized are called to grow into such prayer, into a heart-to-heart intimacy with the God who dwells in our hearts by grace. The loving awareness of his Presence in us is (or should be) the normal course of development for the Christian heart.

---

57. Saint John Cassian, *Conferences*, trans. Boniface Ramsey, O.P. (New York: Newman Press, 1997), 45.

The ultimate example of purity of heart, after Jesus Christ himself, is the Blessed Virgin Mary. The Church teaches that she never consented to either a mortal or a venial sin even once over the whole course of her life (CCC 493). Her heart was simply a burning furnace of love for God and neighbor. Her tenderness and compassion were incomparable, and so too was her contemplative prayer.[58] For she enjoyed a special *fullness of grace* (see Lk 1:28). Though no one else less than Jesus Christ himself ever enjoyed such purity of heart as Mary, such a grace was given to her for you and me. She is the spiritual mother of all, and she is at our service with her exceedingly powerful prayers so that each of us might grow in every way in purity of heart and contemplative prayer according to the grace given to each.

Blessed are the peacemakers . . .

Blessed are the peacemakers, for they shall be called sons of God. To work for the resolution of conflict between people is one sense of making peace, but another sense of peacemaking is simply to put things in order. For peace is the tranquility of order. In order to establish a new and supernatural order in our hearts, Jesus Christ came preaching peace to you who were far off and peace to those who are near (see Eph 2:17). After triumphing over death and rising up from the great abyss, his greeting was simple: "Peace be with you" (Jn 20:19). The Lord Jesus is the ultimate peacemaker. For he pours forth

---

58. In *Rosarium Virginis Mariae*, Pope Saint John Paul II offers a profound reflection on Mary's contemplation (See no. 10).

the Spirit upon us now from the Father's house, and the Spirit moves us from within to practice the beatitudes.

Each beatitude in its own way is a work of peace. In the first three beatitudes, you and I begin to be peacemakers by working for a healthy and holy order in ourselves, in our own self-understanding, passions, and desires. In the subsequent two beatitudes, we become peacemakers still more by working for justice between people and practicing works of mercy. In the beatitude of purity of heart, however, we come to a place of even more profound inner peace. For purity of heart is freedom from all disordered intentions and a fullness of love for God and neighbor. Just as a mountain lake at midnight reflects the light of many stars in complete calm, so a pure heart reflects the light of many graces in profound tranquility.

"Be still, and know that I am God" (Ps 46:10). For Jesus Christ himself is "the hidden man of the heart" in each of the baptized (1 Pet 3:4).[59] He has shared his eternal Sonship with us not only in theory but in practice—the practice of the Beatitudes. The grace of adoption, the grace of becoming one spirit with him in love, flourishes the most in "a gentle and quiet spirit" (1 Pet 3:4). In the Gospels, does Jesus ever seem to be in a frenzy? Does he jump around from here to there impulsively? His disciples were terrified as they tossed around on the boat amid a storm at sea, but Jesus enjoyed such tranquility of heart that he was sound asleep (see Mt 8:23–27). One word from him stilled the waters to "a great calm" (Mt 8:26). He seeks to live the same way in your soul and mine by walking us through the Beatitudes.

---

59. Translation by author.

"Be at peace with yourself, and heaven and earth will be at peace with you," said Saint Isaac of Nineveh.[60] Saint Isaac belonged to the eastern tradition of monasticism in the Church. The eastern monks have always emphasized the value of interior silence, stillness, and tranquility of heart. Such things are not a luxury, but a necessity for deep prayer, conscious union with God, and growing in the awareness of his Presence. Saint Isaac and others like him tell us that by walking the pathways of ascesis—step by step through mourning, meekness, hungering and thirsting for righteousness, showing mercy to all, and growing in purity of heart—there is a peace one comes to experience far beyond all words to describe: "the peace of God that surpasses all understanding" (Phil 4:7 NABRE). Something of the peace of heaven touches the heart even here below.

Blessed are those who are persecuted for the sake of righteousness . . .

Blessed are those who are persecuted for the sake of righteousness, for theirs is the kingdom of heaven. The last Beatitude means that those who are the adopted sons and daughters of God shall also share the fate of Jesus Christ himself. For he is the eternal Son of God, and he was opposed for telling the truth of who he is. In his testimony before Pontius Pilate, Christ "made the good confession" (1 Tim 6:13). Likewise, when the high priest asked him, "Are you the Messiah, the son of the Blessed One?"

---

60. Isaac of Nineveh, *On Ascetical Life*, trans. Mary Hansbury (New York: St. Vladimir's Seminary Press, 1989), 34.

Jesus did not hold back, but said plainly, "I am; and 'you will see the Son of Man / seated at the right hand of the Power / and coming with the clouds of heaven.'" (Mk 14:61–62 NABRE). You and I, too, are called to say out loud to people that Jesus of Nazareth is the eternal Son of God.

Many Catholics say they would rather let their actions bear witness instead of having to speak the words themselves. Although the witness of action is essential and of great value, the Church has warned us that the witness of action is not enough. Pope Paul VI put it this way:

> Even the finest witness will prove ineffective in the long run if it is not explained, justified . . . and made explicit by a clear and unequivocal proclamation of the Lord Jesus. The Good News proclaimed by the witness of life sooner or later has to be proclaimed by the word of life. There is no true evangelization if the name, the teaching, the life, the promises, the kingdom and the mystery of Jesus of Nazareth, the Son of God, are not proclaimed.[61]

It is not enough to bear witness to Jesus Christ with deeds alone. It is essential to bear witness with words. It is necessary to affirm, out loud and unequivocally, that Jesus of Nazareth is the one true savior of the world, and "there is salvation in no one else, for there is no other name under heaven given among men by which we must be saved" (Acts 4:12).

What is needed is the grace of a loud witness in both words and deeds. Perhaps we tremble to testify to Christ,

---

61. Pope Saint Paul VI, *Evangelii Nuntiandi*, The Holy See, December 8, 1975, no. 22, https://www.vatican.va/content/paul-vi/en/apost_exhortations/documents/hf_p-vi_exh_19751208_evangelii-nuntiandi.html.

because we have a sense that to be Christian has become seriously offensive once again. In the first Eucharistic Prayer at Mass, the Roman Canon, the Church lifts up an amazing prayer:

> "To us also, your servants, who though sinners, hope in your abundant mercies, graciously grant some share and fellowship with your holy Apostles and Martyrs: John the Baptist, Stephen, Matthias, Barnabas, Ignatius, Alexander, Marcellinus, Peter, Felicity, Perpetua, Agatha, Lucy, Agnes, Cecilia, Anastasia, and all your Saints."[62]

All the people on this list were seriously offensive to the Roman society of their day. All of them suffered immensely and died for their witness to Jesus. The people who persecuted them did not necessarily have a problem with Jesus. As far as the pagan Romans were concerned, Jesus was nowhere to be seen. The Romans had a problem with them—the Christians. Yet the martyrs cared not for human respect, and they persisted in their witness to the end. For they looked forward to a better home: to the Father's House in the heavenly places. In the first Eucharistic prayer, the Church actually asks for us to share in the grace of the apostles and martyrs. It is a prayer for our fears to be subdued, our testimony to be bold, and our hearts to be fixed on higher and better things—eternal things. All our hopes and desires for things eternal are fulfilled in the Father's House—the topic of the final two chapters.

---

62. "Eucharistic Prayer I (The Roman Canon)," in *The Roman Missal*, 3rd typical ed. (New Jersey: Catholic Book Publishing, 2021), 494.

CHAPTER SEVEN

The Father's House

"IN MY FATHER'S House are many rooms; if it were not so, would I have told you that I go to prepare a place for you? And when I go and prepare a place for you, I will come again and will take you to myself, that where I am you may be also" (Jn 14:2–3). Jesus Christ came into this world in order to lead us to his Father. Just as a man at a social gathering might take a friend and lead him across the room to introduce him to someone else, so the Lord Jesus comes into our world, takes you and me by hand, and leads us beyond the whole world of nature to introduce us to his Father. Yet introductions are just the beginning. The point is to bring us home to the Father's House in the heavenly places for all eternity.

Who is God the Father? One might imagine the most tender, most affectionate, most compassionate, most protective, most supportive, and most loving father ever to walk the face of the earth. One might imagine him reaching down and lifting up his child close to his heart. Such a picture has its truth, but it falls far short of the eternal Father—infinitely short. For the Father of our Lord Jesus Christ is not one of the fathers of this world. He is, rather, the "Father of lights" from whom the world itself flows—the one from whom every good endowment and every perfect gift comes down from above (see Jas 1:17). Your life is his gift to you, and so too is all the knowledge, love, freedom, dignity, and worth you have as a human being. So too are the three great questions you carry in the depths of your heart. God wrote them into your heart precisely in order to answer them, and to answer them in a manner far beyond all you could ever ask or imagine (see Eph 3:20).

The Father's House is a rich mystery indeed, a supernatural mystery, and no one can tell the whole of it except God. For it reveals the ultimate truth of why you and I were created, who you and I are called to be, and how you and I will find the eternal Love that our hearts desire.

Difficulties of Calling God "Father"

Some people struggle with analogies comparing God and human fathers. Some even protest in principle to calling God by the name of "father." Experience of human fatherhood is not always good in a fallen world, in a world still commonly afflicted with the pathos of the heart, in a world still awaiting further healing and renewal of hearts by grace. Those who have first-hand experience of disrespectful, violent, or abusive fathers—or disrespectful and violent men more generally— might seriously struggle with all talk of God as "Father." The difficulties are understandable, and not to be dismissed flippantly. Many people, perhaps, need to hear that the Father's House is *not* like the house of their earthly father—the place where they grew up—especially if they grew up in a toxic home full of violence and abuse.

Horrible experiences of horrible fathers, however, is not the last word on fatherhood. Even if you have had a poor experience (or no experience) of earthly fatherhood, there is still a way to come to know the heavenly Father. Supernatural mysteries are hard to put into words, but with Scripture and tradition to guide us there is a way to catch a glimpse of the supernatural mystery of the Fatherhood of God—a way even for those who have suffered much under their earthly fathers. Knowing full well the difficulties humans often have with earthly fathers, the Lord Jesus taught us to call God "Our Father" (Mt 6:9). The Lord also told us, "I am going to my Father and your Father, to my God and your God" (Jn 20:17 NABRE). He will come back to get us and bring us back to "my Father's House" (Jn 14:2). In the spirit of his universal love for mankind, the Lord is ever at work in our lives to bring us there (see Wis 1:6, Tit 3:4). When we learn to interpret such statements of Scripture aright, we can come to realize that God is not an earthly father, but a mystery of divine Fatherhood—a mystery of divine Light and Love—that is simply all-surpassing.

The Father's House in the Old Testament

"In my Father's House are many rooms" (Jn 14:2). The Lord spoke these words at the Last Supper. He was a Jewish man speaking to other Jewish men, and in their minds the expression *father's house* had a rich and definite meaning.[63] In ancient Israel, the primary figure in a *father's house* was the oldest living male ancestor. The household included all his sons and grandsons, their wives, daughters, and slaves or indentured servants. Such a unit typically consisted of anywhere from fifty to one hundred people. The oldest male ancestor was simply called "the father." The father had authority over all members of his house. In ancient Hebrew, there were words for aunt and uncle, but the words for brother and sister extended to both immediate siblings and cousins, and there was not even a word for the latter.[64] In such a father's house, the role of the father was very rich.

The first role of the father was to supply material sustenance and wealth. Land and livestock were the main forms of wealth, and inheritance was more or less the only way anyone received any of it. Individuals as such could not really generate wealth, and people were not able simply to go out and get a job. This is why in the parable of the prodigal son, after the son took his share of the inheritance and

---

63. The following meditations on Jewish family life are based on the following sources: Roland de Vaux, *Ancient Israel: Its Life and Institutions*, trans. John McHugh (New York: McGraw Hill, 1961); C.J.H. Wright, "Family," in *The Anchor Bible Dictionary*, ed. Noel Freedman, vol. 2, D-G (New York: Doubleday, 1992), 761–779; J. Daane, "Father," in *The International Standard Bible Encyclopedia*, vol. 2 (Grand Rapids, MI: Eerdmans, 1982), 284–286; J. E. Hartley, "Father's House," in *The International Standard Bible Encyclopedia*, vol. II (Grand Rapids, MI: Eerdmans, 1982), 286–287; Paul W. Miller, *Calling God "Father": Essays on the Bible, Fatherhood, and Culture* (New York: Paulist Press, 1999).

64. See Wright, "Family," 762.

squandered it, all that remained was to sell himself into servitude to another house. There were no companies around. There were only other houses of other fathers. The father's house was the basic economic unit of society. If you had a father, you had your material needs supplied. If you did not have a father, you had virtually nothing. That is why the Old Testament prophets show particular concern for the plight of widows and orphans.

The second role of the father was to settle questions of justice. The father's house was something like a court. It was the forum in which all grievances between the members were settled. Grievances against another were brought to the father, and the matter was settled by his decision. All members of the father's house were subject to his authority, even adult males with children of their own, and there was no higher court of appeal. We see something like this playing out at the end of the parable of the prodigal son, when the older brother brings his case against the younger brother to the father (see Lk 15:25–32). If you had a father, then you had someone to secure your due under justice. But if you had no father, who would stand up for your due and see to your vindication?

The third role of the father was to provide protection. His house formed a military unit. All of the able-bodied men in the house were called up against raids and invasions. The brothers of David, for example, went off to battle the Philistines. After David came of age, he joined his brothers on the front line (see 1 Sam 17). Later, the Maccabeans carried on their campaign as a warrior-family against the Greeks (see 1 and 2 Mac). The ancient world was a hostile one, full of raids and invasions out of nowhere. If you had a father, you were protected and safe. If you did not have a father, you were vulnerable and consistently exposed to threats.

The fourth role of the father was to teach the truth to his house. The father's house was the place where the traditions of Israel and the terms of the covenants were handed on. It was the father who was responsible for teaching the Torah to his sons, and the Torah prescribes in detail what the father is to do in leading the Passover. The whole of Psalm 78 is a celebration of fatherly education into the story of Israel. Verses 3 and 4 sing of "things that we have heard and known, / that our fathers have told us. / We will not hide them from their children, / but tell to the coming generation" (Ps 78:3–4). Verses 5–6 say still more strongly, "He commanded our fathers / to teach to their children; / that the next generation might know them, / the children yet unborn." The remainder of the Psalm goes on to do exactly that—to retell the story of Israel in verse. If you had a father, you had someone to tell you the meaning and ultimate truth of the world. If you had no father, how would you ever learn the meaning or ultimate truth of things?

The fifth role of the father, if it can be called a role, was simply to love the members of his house. According to various experts, among the ancient Jews "fathers came to be involved with their families and their children to a degree unparalleled in other cultures."[65] Though this love and involvement extended to all family members, the father's love played out in a particular way with sons. The literature of gentile pagans all around Israel is filled with stories of violence between fathers

---

65. Miller, *Calling God "Father"*, 70.

and sons and even many tales of patricide. Comparatively speaking, the Old Testament accounts of father-son relationships are rather peaceful, though far from perfect—more below on the problematic side of things. In many ways, the relationships of fathers and sons in Israel were full of loyalty and affection. Biblical scholars speculate about how the experience of fatherhood in Israel came to be so different from that of surrounding cultures, and some answer that the ritual and ceremony of Israel forged a bond between fathers and sons as they did nowhere else.[66]

The redemption of the firstborn sons of Israel is but one example (see Ex 13:13–16; Num 18:15–16). Some scholars surmise how the redemption ceremony might have gone based on how it goes today.[67] The father brought his firstborn son to the synagogue and ceremonially handed the infant boy over to the rabbi. The rabbi then asked the father whether the boy was the father's child. The father answered yes. In order to claim his son back, the father handed some silver coins over to the rabbi. The rabbi then handed the boy back to the father. The son, therefore, knew he had been claimed and purchased at a price by his father. Though one might question how precisely the ceremony transpired in ancient times (the details may have varied and are somewhat lost to history), many contemporary Jews still participate in

---

66. See Miller, ch. 6.

67. See Miller, 58–60. Special thanks also to Tom McCreesh, O.P., Professor of Old Testament at Providence College, and Steven Ryan, O.P., Professor of Old Testament at the Dominican House of Studies, for their enlightening remarks about the redemption of the firstborn in ancient Israel.

a similar practice. It teaches a universal and essential truth of fatherhood. Real fathers claim their children, and out of love pay the price for them.

The discussion of the role of fathers in ancient Israel is inspirational to many people, especially men today who want to know how to be fathers. The five roles of fathers are permanent lessons for what fathers should be, even though fathers today should enact them in a different manner— different for the better in many ways. For family life in ancient Israel was not idyllic. Although Israelite family life was remarkably different from that of pagan societies, even in Israel many fathers and their families had grave problems. The genealogies of the Lord in the Gospels of Matthew 1:1–17 and Luke 3:23–38, for example, include the names of fathers who were disasters by any set of standards. The eternal Son of God chose to become incarnate in a family line riddled with seriously dysfunctional fathers. Saint Joseph, a true Israelite and Son of David in his own right, was exceptional in more ways than one.

Some also might be wondering how the account of the father's house in ancient Israel applies to women. The question is large, and the answer will unfold gradually. To begin, the purpose of learning about the father's house in ancient Israel is not to glorify ancient patriarchal social structures. Such structures belong to an era and stage of divine revelation that is now over. For Jesus Christ has come to reveal still greater and more perfect mysteries to us—mysteries such as *his* Father's House (see Heb 9:11). The father's houses of ancient Israel were *prefigurations* of the Father's House revealed to us by Jesus Christ, and as prefigurations they serve to illustrate and help us understand the mystery of the Father's House. One particular example is worth noting. Fathers in ancient Israel did not normally extend an inheritance to their daughters, but the Old Testament records one important exception. Job, the man of suffering, left an inheritance to his daughters (see Job 42:15). His action was significant and prefigured something greater yet to come for all women through another man of suffering: Jesus Christ.

In ancient Israel, the father's house was a complete form of life. It was, in effect, a small business, a national guard unit, a people's court, a local parish, a school, and a home all in one. It was the basic unit of social life and total in its scope. In the father's house was everything a human being needs—all the necessities and blessings of life and prosperity. In fact, in ancient Hebrew, there is not even a single word for *family*. In Hebrew, the only expression referring to family is *father's house*.[68] So, when the Lord said to the Twelve, "In my Father's House there are many rooms, and I go to prepare a place for you," how would the Twelve have understood him? They would have understood him to be saying something like this: *I have a Father, and therefore, I have it all. I have everything you or anyone could ever need or want. I am opening it all up to you now and bringing you into it. In the abundance of my life with the Father, I am making a place for you. All of it is yours. My whole life with the Father is yours.*

---

68. Wright, "Family," 761–779.

The Father's House in the New Testament

When standing before Pilate, Jesus said to him, "My kingdom is not of this world" (Jn 18:36).[69] The Lord might also have said his Father's House is not of this world. It would have been true, but it would have made less sense to a Gentile politician. The Twelve, on the other hand, had an idea of what Jesus meant by "Father's house" but needed clarification about the kingdom of God. Even as Christ was about to ascend, his disciples still thought the kingdom was simply an earthly, temporal form of kingship (see Acts 1:6). It would take the gift of the Spirit at Pentecost to illuminate and clarify for them what the kingdom of God really is.

Just as the Twelve needed a special illumination of the Spirit to realize and understand that the kingdom of God is not an earthly one but a mystery of the supernatural order, so you and I need a special illumination of the Spirit to realize and understand how the Father's House is not an ancient patriarchal structure, or an abusive childhood home, or any social structure of the natural order at all. It is a theological mystery. Jesus alone can teach it to us. For he alone knows it. It is his "family of origin," so to speak, in the God who dwells in unapproachable light (see 1 Tim 6:16). It might help to recall here the Rublev icon of the Trinity as a sort of window into heaven.

Though the Father's House is an all-surpassing mystery, it is possible for faith to learn something of the Father's

---

69. Translation by author.

House by comparing and contrasting it with a father's house of the ancient Israelite kind. Both the similarities and the differences serve to illustrate the Father's House of the supernatural order. In this way, even those who have personally experienced next to nothing of good earthly fatherhood can catch a glimpse of the Father of lights and come to know by faith something of his wonderful love for us. Let us begin with the redemption ceremony.

Just as the fathers of ancient Israel loved their firstborn sons, claimed them, and paid a price for them in the redemption ceremony, so has the eternal Father done for you and me—men and women alike—regardless of our birth order in our natural families. "For God so loved the world that he gave his only Son, so that everyone who believes in him might not perish but might have eternal life" (Jn 3:16 NABRE). Good Friday was a redemption ceremony. That day is called good because the Father claimed Adam—the whole of humanity—at a price. The Father did not mete out a few coins for us, but handed over his only begotten Son Jesus in bloodshed. "Having loved his own who were in the world, he loved them to the end" (Jn 13:1). Every one of us can know now that you and I have been purchased at a price—at the price of the cross. Truly, there are no words on earth great enough to celebrate how our Father has loved us. "To ransom a slave, you gave away your Son."[70]

---

70. "The Easter Proclamation (Exsultet)," in the *Roman Missal*, 3rd typical ed. (New Jersey: Catholic Book Publishing, 2021), 208.

On Easter Sunday, however, Jesus Christ rose from the dead. In so doing, he shattered the permanence of death and removed its sting. When he ascended, the Lord Jesus passed body and soul through the door of the Father's House in the heavenly places. The point is for us to follow him there until we too enter into that bright place, and God has given us his Spirit and his Church to lead us there every step of the way.

Furthermore, just as the fathers of ancient Israel taught the members of their houses the truth of what life is all about, so too does the Father of lights teach us. Again, he does so in a much higher and more exalted way, not only for sons but for all. The Father, working together with the Son and Spirit, has given us the divinely inspired testimony of the prophets and apostles, and their testimony comes down to us in the Scripture and tradition of the Church. It is the testimony of God. Through it, you and I can learn the truth that really saves our souls—the same truth the Twelve learned from Jesus Christ himself. The Spirit given to the Church continually protects and clarifies what the testimony means, indeed, lights up for us the meaning of all things. For centuries the popes, bishops, and doctors of Church have labored with the help of the Spirit to guard, communicate, and clarify what God has revealed. As a result, we can learn answers to the deepest questions of life, understand something of the pathos of the heart, and learn to walk the way of friendship together in the Spirit and in the Church. We learn gradually how to follow the law of love and to practice the Beatitudes. We learn repentance and conversion of heart little by little each day, and in so doing, you and I come to understand the purpose of our lives, the identity the Father has for each of us, and how to give and receive his love.

Just as the fathers of ancient Israel settled questions of justice between the members of their house, so the Father of our Lord Jesus Christ settles questions of justice among all human beings, but in a manner far surpassing the fathers of ancient Israel or any human system of justice. For God is good and "desires everyone to be saved" (1 Tim 2:4 NRSV). He has given us all our being and our life, and created us all in his image. He established the first human beings in a state of original justice, but on account of the fall the human race has become rather unruly. All are afflicted with the pathos of the heart. Yet the good God was unwilling simply to watch his creation waste away. So, in order to establish a new and supernatural order among the persons whom he created, an order perfectly realized nowhere except in his House in the heavenly places, the Father has sent his eternal Son into the world to die on the cross for us and has poured out his Holy Spirit upon all human beings. Through the voice of Christ, the preaching of the Church, and the whispers of conscience, God calls all people to repent of all their sins and to receive forgiveness and new life from him.

For as we said in Chapter One, God has given to all people at least *some* knowledge of his existence and attributes through the many signs of him in nature. Furthermore, as we said in Chapter Two, all people know there is a higher law and know something of it, at least to some extent. All human beings have at least some knowledge of good and evil, right and wrong. Still more, as we said in Chapter Three, all people receive at least some grace from God. There is no one on earth whose life is simply untouched by grace. He gives the light of many graces to all. Human beings, therefore, are responsible before God, according to the lights and graces given to each, for every freely chosen thought, word, and deed of our lives. Given God's desire to save all, and the responsibility of all people before him, the Church teaches that in his mercy God gives to all people grace sufficient for their salvation, even if in many cases the manner in which he does so is known only to himself.[71] Truly, he extends mercy and grace to all.

At the moment of death—at the threshold, so to speak, of the Father's house in the heavenly places—every human being passes through a moment traditionally called the *particular judgment*. Just how the event shall transpire for each one of us is hard to say in any detail. But in that moment the stance of the soul toward God, in this life and especially at the moment of death, shall be laid open. Those who in this life accepted the grace of God, repented of all their sins, and had God as their first love above all things—at least at the moment of death—shall pass through their particular judgment without condemnation and go into the Father's House.[72] But those

---

71. "Since Christ died for all, and since all men are in fact called to one and the same destiny, which is divine, we must hold that the Holy Spirit offers to all the possibility of being made partakers, in a way known to God, of the Paschal mystery" (*Gaudium et Spes*, no. 22.5 as quoted in CCC 1260. cf. *Lumen Gentium*, no. 16; *Ad Gentes*, no. 7).

72. On the way into the Father's House they shall pass through purgatory as well *unless* all the temporal consequences of their sins have first been remedied through suitable penance or indulgences. Purgatory, penances, and indulgences, however, are topics deserving a fuller explanation elsewhere.

who die with mortal sin on their souls, who did not repent of their sins at least by the moment of death, who did not have God as their first love above all things shall—freely and of their own accord—forever flee the Light of God. For a mortal sin on the soul, so long as one has not repented of it, is essentially an interior condition of *aversion from God*. Repentance alone changes the soul from having such an aversion to God to loving him above all things. Repentance, therefore, is the key to entry into the Father's House in the heavenly places. Repentance is not possible after death, but only in this life.[73] "Now is the acceptable time," Scripture says (2 Cor 6:2). Through the particular judgment of each person, God shall adequately settle the question of justice regarding all the free choices of all people of all times and places of history and render to all according as their deeds deserve (see Rom 2:6; Rev 22:12).[74]

Just as a father in ancient Israel provided protection, and his whole house was a military unit, so our eternal Father protects us in the warfare that is now ours. As we make our way from life on earth to the Father's House in the heavenly places, there is a warfare to be endured. It is not a war in the

---

73. According to the teaching of the Church, the opportunity for repentance belongs to this life only. There is no second chance after death. CCC 1021: "Death puts an end to human life as the time open to either accepting or rejecting the divine grace manifested in Christ."

74. God shall also address sin, and the whole problem of evil generally, through the second coming of Christ, the general judgment, and the final purification of the world at the end, but the mysteries of the end deserve another treatment all their own.

earthly sense of armed combat. "For we are not contending against flesh and blood, but against the principalities, against the powers, against the world rulers of this present darkness, against the spiritual hosts of wickedness in the heavenly places" (Eph 6:12). On the way to the Father's House on high, the battle here below consists of dealing daily with *logismoi*, temptations, and the lures of this passing world. Every step of the way, the Father protects us in a particular way. He knows the needs of each and does not allow anyone to be tempted beyond his or her strength (see 1 Cor 10:13). Instead, he gives us graces of vigilance and prayer and the grace to resist temptation. The Father also sends guardian angels to protect us and establishes ministers in the Church who serve to disentangle us from evil in various ways. Each of us, therefore, can truly say: "Even though I walk through the valley of the shadow of death, / I will fear no evil, for you are with me" (Ps 23:4 NABRE). In the end, once we have passed through death and our particular judgment, and hopefully gone into that bright place on high, there shall be no more threat of evil or even the slightest hostilities. There, all shall be peace.

Finally, just as the sons of a father's house in Israel received an inheritance from the father, so you and I have an inheritance coming to us from the Father of Jesus Christ in the heavenly places. The members of an earthly father's house received an earthly inheritance, but you and I have a heavenly inheritance awaiting us with the heavenly Father. Our inheritance is not one of land, livestock, or temporal goods. It is "the inheritance of the saints in light" (Col 1:12). The "inheritance of the saints" is first of all God himself. Grace, in the primary sense of the term, is God's gift of himself to us. Grace in this sense is God saying, "I am yours."[75] Yet, when he shares himself with us, he also shares with us all who belong to him by grace. The inheritance, therefore, is really the whole communion of saints. Whatever God gave to the saints, all graces of all times and places, was given to them to be shared with *you*. You might think of your favorite saint. Now, in the Father's house, the saint's attitude toward you is: "All the grace I ever received was given to me for you. I am for you." The Virgin Mary says the same to you, Saint Joseph does too, and all the apostles, martyrs, and doctors of the Church as well. Unlike the inheritance in ancient Israel, this inheritance is not for sons alone. Rather, what was the exception with Job has become the norm in Jesus Christ. Women who are baptized into Christ—daughters of the Father—now also receive a share in the inheritance. For in Christ there is "neither male nor female" (Gal 3:28).

Heaven Touches the Earth

How shall we sum up the supernatural mystery of the Father's House? The whole journey of the Christian life, the whole way of friendship with Jesus Christ in the Church, is meant to take us there. In one sense, the Father's House is the entire Holy Trinity. For the Son and the Spirit proceed from

---

75. See CCC 1999 and 2003.

the Father and take their origin from him. Rublev's icon of
the Trinity, therefore, is something of a window into the
Father's House. In another sense, the Father's House is the
whole of heaven: the Holy Trinity, the Virgin Mary, the holy
angels, and all the saints together. It is the *communio* of all in
the heavenly places, in the state of final perfection, in the state
of flourishing without fail as they abide in the Light.

In another sense, the Father's House is something more
familiar to us—already at hand. It is something we can experience to some extent here below while we are still on the way to
the heavenly places. It is the great *communio* of the Church on
earth. The Church on earth, properly speaking, is the *sacrament* of the Father's House. To call the Church a sacrament of
the Father's House is to say the Church is a *sign* of the eternal
abode with the Father as well as the present and active *cause* of
our progress to that bright place. The Father's House as a
whole, therefore, is a supernatural mystery of something—
Someone—up above touching us here below and drawing us
upward so "that where I am you may be also" (Jn 14:3).

At the beginning of this chapter, we said that to understand the heavenly Father one might think of the most loving
of human fathers lifting up his child and holding the child
over his heart. We said that such a picture has its truth, but
needs to be qualified. This whole chapter has qualified it. Now
we are in a position to say that the Father does indeed do
something similar with you and me, but in a manner much
more mysterious and metaphysical than one might at first
think. He uses the whole Church, all her teachings and sacraments, all the practicals of the way, and all events of our lives

to lift us up to his heart—the heart of our Father. In the next and last chapter, we will learn more deeply how God brings us into his life through adoption by grace and grants us to know something of his Love.

CHAPTER EIGHT

The Mystery of Filial Adoption

ALL THE PREVIOUS chapters have been an extended meditation on the mystery of our adoption by grace—what it is and how to live it. The word adoption has rarely been used, but all our points have touched on the topic in one way or another. In our Baptism, by sheer grace, you and I were adopted into God. That means we have become participants in the life of the Holy Trinity. We have become a temple of the Spirit of Love, another Christ in the world, and we look to the Father of lights for everything. Yet, having acquired an overview of our adoption by grace, we can now gain a still deeper understanding of it. What precisely is the meaning of being adopted into God by grace? How might you and I come to know the Father personally for ourselves? How does the Father's House in heaven touch us on the earth even now and draw us upward?

The Grace of Adoption

In our Baptism, God has given us the grace of "adoption as sons" (Gal 4:5). To understand the expression, let us consider what takes place in adoptions. Adoptions of the ordinary human kind are established by a legal transaction. The adopted child becomes the legal son or daughter of the adoptive parents. For better or for worse, their home—with all of its love, safety, support, and stability, or lack thereof—is now the child's home too. Its influence on the child runs deep. Nonetheless, the adopted son or daughter is not of the same flesh and blood as the adoptive parents.

Our adoption into God by grace, however, differs from adoptions of the ordinary human kind. It is not established by a legal transaction. Rather, in our Baptism God pours his Spirit into our spirits in a manner far beyond anything humans could ever do with one another by nature. In our Baptism, God also transmits to your soul and mine something of the eternal Son's own relationship with the Father within the Trinity itself—a true participation in the eternal Sonship of the Son. As a result, each of us has a relationship with the Father, but it is not merely your individual relationship or mine. Rather, by the grace of adoption you and I have something of *Christ's own* relationship with the Father (see Rom 8:15; Gal 4:6). To put it another way, Christ has opened up his relationship with the Father to you and me and incorporated us into it, and now you and I share in it. "In that day you will know that I am in my Father, and you in me, and I in you," says the Lord (Jn 14:20).

Our calling as the children of God by grace is to learn how to relate to the Father from out of the Son's own relationship with him. Scripture describes our share in that relationship in terms of living in our own hearts the *prayer* of Jesus to the Father. What could be closer to someone's spirit, what could be more personal, than the most intimate prayer of the person's heart? Scripture tells us the most intimate prayer of the heart of Christ was "*Abba*" (Mk 14:36, emphasis added). To call God by the name of *Abba* or *Father* was unprecedented in Israel. Jesus' praying in such personal and familiar terms to God was truly new. It was *his* personal prayer. It was original and unique to his heart. Yet, in his unfathomable love for us, it also pleased him to share his prayer with us. He wants you and me to call upon his Father too, and to do so also in his Spirit. For this reason, when God poured out his Spirit upon the first Christians, something momentous began in their hearts. The most intimate prayer of the heart of Jesus began welling up in their own hearts too: "You have received the Spirit of sonship through which *we* cry '*Abba*!'" (Rom 8:15, emphasis added).[76]

Thanks to the grace of adoption, the prayer life of Jesus Christ is going on in the depths of your heart. Your prayer life and the prayer life of Jesus Christ are one—a common life between you and God. To put it another way, the risen Lord Jesus now lives and enacts his prayer to the Father through you and me. It all takes place in the depths of our hearts, and

---

76. Translation by author.

it takes place in the depths of the Spirit whose temple we have become. You and I have been so loved by God, so drawn into God, so united with God that something of the prayer life of heaven itself has begun in our souls and expands in us through prayer. In the beginning of the spiritual life, you and I might not sense anything special taking place, but something special has begun by grace. It is a matter of faith. The more we believe in the reality of the prayer of Christ taking place in our hearts, the more we can awaken to it and come to live it more consciously. The more we come to accept by faith the reality that we are adopted by grace, and that the eternal Father gazes upon us with love as his own dearly beloved sons and daughters in Christ, the more deeply we can enter into contemplative prayer.

The Call to Contemplative Prayer

All Christians are called to have the eyes of their hearts enlightened so that you and I may know what is the hope that belongs to our call (see Eph 1:18). God created the eyes of our hearts so that we might come to know him, but, as we have previously discussed, the eyes of our hearts are afflicted in many ways on account of the fall. Spiritually speaking, all of us are a bit like the blind men in the Gospels. We need the Lord Jesus to open the eyes of our hearts so that we can come to know the Father's love. Now, it is one thing to hear of the Father's love, another to believe in the Father's love, and another still to experience the Father's love for yourself. By now, you have heard much of the Father's love, and hopefully believe in his love for you personally. One of the frustrations people most commonly express to me, however, is that they want to *know* the Father. They want to somehow go beyond what talks and books tell them *about* the Father, and they want to experience his eternal Love personally for themselves. Often without having the word for it, what they are asking for is contemplative prayer. And it is no surprise they are asking for it. All the faithful are called to contemplative prayer. Yet, how shall we understand such a thing?

The highest and most exalted way to know the Father is simply to go to heaven. There, bathed in the light of his face, we shall enjoy the happy sight of God. In heaven, we will know the Father most deeply, intimately, and personally. Such knowledge goes with the heavenly sight of the entire Holy Trinity—the Father, Son, and Holy Spirit. But do we have to wait for heaven to know the Father so personally and intimately? Not necessarily. Contemplative prayer is like a point halfway between earth and heaven. It is based upon hearing of the Father and believing in his love, but it rises to something more. What happens in contemplative prayer is that one begins to enjoy a deeper perception and higher awareness of God. This deeper perception and higher awareness is more than hearsay knowledge of the Father, but it is less than the happy sight of God in heaven. It is, rather, an enigmatic perception of the Most High (see 1 Cor 13:12). It is a sense of his Presence dwelling in our hearts and working all around us in a thousand ways. Such an enigmatic perception of God is possible even here below, in this life, and it is truly a ray of the divine Light shining in our hearts to give us a knowledge of his glory shining on the face of Jesus Christ (see 2 Cor 4:6).

Contemplative prayer is not for a few special people but for all the baptized faithful. It is the ordinary fruit of our participation by grace in the personal prayer of Jesus Christ. If anyone should ask how to enter into contemplative prayer, the answer is that we grow into it gradually by walking the way of friendship. Believing in his Love, watching and praying, doing good to all, and practicing the Beatitudes are all part of the road to contemplative prayer. The road is challenging. It calls for walking away from the many false allurements of this world. It calls for being emptied of every intention toward deadly sin. It calls for humble dependence on God in the face of all the empty show of the devil. Growing into contemplative prayer requires a change of heart and of habits. The necessary changes run deep. In the process, you and I shall surely suffer a thousand trials and difficulties, perhaps even to the point of being "struck down, but not destroyed" (2 Cor 4:9). For the way of friendship, and the road to contemplative prayer, is also the way of the cross. The Lord calls us to take up our cross daily and follow him (see Lk 9:23). Yet, through it all, God readies our hearts for the grace of contemplative prayer.

Contemplative prayer does not consist of visions or private revelations or similar spectacular phenomena. It is more like being in love. The lover is captivated by the beloved, and the beloved by the Lover. A contemplative soul is captivated by God. The eyes of your heart gradually become more intent on God. As the grace of God grows in your heart, your glance upon God tends to simplify, your love for God tends to burn more ardently, and your heart's sense of his Presence tends to become more vivid. His Presence becomes your all.

Regardless of where you are today, whether you have a sense of his Presence or not, the truth is that the Father loves you. His eyes of love have been upon you your whole life long. He loved you from before the foundation of the world and has given you life in the days of time. From the first moment of your existence until now, he has gazed upon you with total love. The Father has supported you through every difficulty and trial and directed every one of your steps according to eternal designs. Even your missteps do not change his Love. Like the father of the prodigal son, the Father loves you with a merciful love that is greater than all your mistakes and sins, and he is eager to embrace you after a fall and celebrate your return (see Lk 15:11–32). He will always be there for you, no matter what may come in your life. Your future belongs to the Father. So, too, the future of the world. The more we take such truths to heart, believe in the Father, and lift up our hearts to the Father with whatever trust and love we have today, the more we shall really enter into contemplative prayer.

Living the Mystery

All the practicals of the way of friendship lead to contemplative prayer, but we know that something greater than contemplative prayer has been given to us from the Father's House. There is an *actual reality* on the earth today from the Father's House in the heavenly places. It is the Eucharist. For many of us, going to Mass, or the Divine Liturgy, might seem like just another merely human ritual or cultural event, but nothing could be farther from the truth. In all of the sacraments of the Church, heaven touches men and women on

earth in a powerful way, but in the Eucharist the man of
heaven is actually present with us in person. In the liturgy, the
Lord Jesus Christ does something amazing. How, then, shall
we understand what is really going on in the celebration of the
Eucharist?

On Good Friday, Jesus offered himself to the Father in
love once and for all. Even in death his offering did not cease,
and he has never taken it back. Therefore, he continues to
offer himself to the Father in love even now, but in a different
condition than on Good Friday. Ever since his ascension, he
now stands before the Father in the eternal sanctuary, offering
himself to the Father in the light of heaven. Jesus shows his
glorified wounds to the Father and intercedes for us. In this
way, Jesus is the eternal high priest over the house of God (see
Heb 10:21), and without leaving his place in glory he is also
now the principal celebrant of every one of our liturgical cel-
ebrations in the Church on the earth today.

How? In each and every Mass, the priest is his delegate,
but in a manner that is more than merely legal. The priest is a
living icon of Christ as Head of the Church. For at the ordination of the priest, he was permanently sealed in the depths of
his soul in a special way. Thanks to the seal on the priest's soul,
the eternal high priest in heaven now works through the priest
on earth to change things. When the priest takes bread in his
hands and pronounces the words, "This is my body," the bread
ceases to be bread and is now the body of Christ himself. And
when the priest takes the chalice of wine in his hands and says,
"This is the chalice of my blood," the wine ceases to be wine
and is now the blood of Christ himself. Through the words of
the priest, Jesus Christ himself is truly present on the altar,

not merely in the form of symbols without the substance of Christ, but in his full reality as God-Man. After the priest pronounces the words of consecration, the Eucharist looks like bread and tastes like bread, but it is not bread. The Eucharist looks like wine and tastes like wine, but it is not wine. For Jesus Christ is now truly present, body, blood, soul, and divinity, in the Eucharist. The Eucharist is the Lord Jesus Christ himself, the man of heaven, wholly present in our midst. He is present in a special and unique way, to be sure, but his presence is as real as can be.

The people, too, have an important part to play in the celebration. For in our Baptism every one of us received a seal on our souls as well, not the same sort of seal the priest received in his ordination, but a most important one nonetheless. Thanks to the seal of Baptism, every one of the faithful now has a share in the sonship of Jesus Christ. It bears repeating: you are Jesus. The seal you received on your soul in Baptism is the supernatural ability to receive the grace of God in all the other sacraments and to join Christ in worshiping the Father in Spirit and in truth at Mass (see Jn 4:24). The priest and people assembled together form the *whole* Christ—head and members in one. In the liturgy, as his Mystical Body, we enact Jesus Christ's own prayer to the Father. Or, rather, Jesus Christ enacts his prayer to the Father through us—through our words, our gestures, and our prayers. His personal prayer to the Father expresses itself publicly at every Mass. You and I are *in it*.

In the Eucharistic Celebration, Jesus Christ offers himself to the Father in love in three different ways. First, Jesus Christ the eternal high priest now offers himself to the Father in the eternal sanctuary. Second, Jesus Christ in the priest on earth now offers Jesus Christ truly present on the altar to the Father. Third, the people unite their hearts to Christ offering himself to the Father. In these ways, the offering takes place both in heaven and on earth. It is all one offering in which Jesus Christ gives *himself* to the Father in heaven through *our* liturgical acts on the earth. Jesus Christ's offering of himself on Calvary once took place in a bloody manner, his offering of himself in heaven now takes place in a glorified manner, and his offering of himself in the Church on earth now takes place in a liturgical manner through ritualized words and gestures. It is all essentially one and the same act of Jesus Christ offering himself to the Father in love. Hence, it is called the holy sacrifice of the Mass.

In Holy Communion, Jesus Christ also gives himself completely to us in love. To receive Holy Communion is to ingest the Life of God. No other blessing is comparable. It is the greatest gift of God's love for us. Our common calling as the adopted children of God is to return love for love received: to give ourselves to God completely and without reserve. "My son, give me your heart" (Prov 23:26). We give our hearts to him in celebrating the Eucharist, but "lift up your hearts" does not end when the Mass ends. For you and I are called to walk all the days of our years here below in the way of friendship with God in the great *communio* of the Church, to lift up our hearts in contemplative prayer, and to look to the Father of lights for every good and perfect gift coming down from above (see Jas 1:17).

The liturgy of the Church is the place where we live the mystery of our adoption to the full. In the liturgy, God gathers his adopted ones together as the Mystical Body of his own Son Jesus Christ, and as his Mystical Body we worship the eternal Father in the Spirit. In this way, even though we are still on the earth, we can live even now something of the Father's House in the heavenly places. The dispositions of the heart proper for entering into the liturgy are those of Jesus Christ himself: thanksgiving, adoration, petition, and reparation for sin. The more the dispositions of his heart become ours, the more our hearts become his. Simply to be there is a gift beyond all telling, but the gift is often lost on us. For the whole truth of what is taking place in the liturgy remains somewhat veiled to our human eyes.

Human beings cannot know what is actually happening in the liturgy either by sensation alone or by natural reason alone. For human sensation and human intelligence are adapted to knowing things of this world, but the Eucharist is not of this world. The many beauties of the world point us upward to God in a thousand ways, but the Eucharist comes down to us from above. It is a reality from the Father's House—from the other side of the veil between our human eyes and the heavenly places. The Eucharist was given to us by the Father's own Son in the flesh. It is a sheer gift. Faith is necessary to realize the reality of the Eucharist and the magnitude of the gift. Faith is necessary to know the whole truth of what goes on in the liturgy of the Church. Only faith can realize that the liturgy is the point of entry on earth today to the Father's House in the heavenly places. The priest, the people, the rites, the words, the gestures, and the appearances of bread and wine: all of it reveals the Father's House to the eyes of loving faith. Loving faith in the whole revelation of

God learns to perceive what is really going on in the liturgy. The liturgy, in turn, can become a place of contemplative prayer—a place where the eternal love of the Father shines in our hearts more and more. On the way to heaven, the liturgy is where we can fully be ourselves as the adopted children of God and learn to be at home in the Trinity.

Conclusion

O VER THE YEARS of traveling and preaching to college students and young adults all over the United States and beyond, and presenting them the good news as it has been set out in this book, one of the most common responses I have received is: "Why has no one ever told me this before?" Young men and women are genuinely surprised to learn that the purpose of their lives is to enter into the Holy Trinity. They are astonished to hear the meaning of their Baptism: *you are Jesus.* They are unaccustomed to hear someone speak of the great *communio* of the Church in which "the love of God has been poured forth in our hearts through the Holy Spirit who has been given to us" (Rom 5:5).[77] Why does all of this sound so *new* to people?

The answer varies. Some people have never received even a basic instruction in the truths of the Gospel. For them, all of

---

77. Translation by author.

it is quite new. Others might have learned the truths of the Gospel in some catechetical form, but their understanding of things never went beyond catechesis. They never came to understand how all the different truths of the Gospel hang together in a single account of what life is all about and how to live it. Some have received a great deal of instruction in how to live, but their formation was centered almost exclusively upon morality, which left them with the impression that Christianity is little more than a bunch of rules, commandments, and prohibitions. Still others think the Gospel has little to do with intelligence, rationality, and the life of the mind. They presume the Gospel has no solid truth in it, no answers to real questions, and no real light to increase our understanding of anything. Perhaps they heard from a Christian, "It's not about reason, but about a relationship," and took what they heard literally. In all of these points of view, one thing or another from the Catholic faith is missing.

The truth coming down to us from the prophets and apostles of old is quite different from what many people understand it to be. The Gospel truth is *catholic* in the original sense of the term: *according to the whole*. The whole Gospel of Jesus Christ speaks deeply to the heart but through the mind. It is rational and explains the truth of what life is all about, who we are, and how to love and be loved, yet it is also relational and teaches us how to walk in the way of friendship with God. It tells us what to do and how to live, but it is not merely a set of rules imposed on us. It acknowledges the reality of the deep heart in each human person, and the pathos of the heart afflicting us all, but it neither excuses people for sin nor leaves them to die in it. For the Gospel is essentially an announcement of the way to healing and transformation of the heart by grace, and the way is ongoing repentance of sin and following Jesus Christ. Jesus Christ is the Teacher, we are his disciples, and he aims to unite us and identify us with himself for supernatural purposes. He wants us to know his Father. The teachings of Jesus Christ are one and all revelations of the Father's Love.

It takes the eyes of the heart, however, a long time to adjust to the Light. By having a loving faith, watching at all times and praying, doing good to all, and practicing the Beatitudes, we actually follow the Lord Jesus to new Life. We follow him from this world to the Father's House in the heavenly places, we follow him in the Church, and we follow him under the influence of the Spirit living and working in our hearts. The Spirit is the one who changes us, carves us into another Christ, every step of the way. The center of our lives on earth is the Eucharist, and our hope is to grow in contemplative prayer—for the eyes of our hearts to be opened to the revelation of the Father's Love.

The saints are the people who confirm the truth of the Gospel and demonstrate in their flesh just how real it all is. True, the Church is a hospital for sinners, but the Church is also the home of the saints. In commenting on the Beatitudes, we found saints to illustrate every one of them. Some were canonized and others were not. Some were ancient, some were contemporary. Along the way in my journeys, I am convinced, I have even met a few saints for myself. You might not marvel if you met them. In one sense they were ordinary people, but in another sense they were extraordinary. They knew their purpose, they knew who they were, and they knew where to find Love. They had come to drink deeply of the Spirit, humbly accepted their true identity in Christ, and remained under the gaze of the Father in their prayer. Even though they still lived on the earth, in a sense their hearts were already at home in the Trinity. The Father's House had become their own, and so it can be for you too. Though your life might be ordinary in many ways, by the grace of God something extraordinary can come to pass in the depths of your heart. You, too, can drink deeply of the Spirit of Love. You, too, can know who you are in Christ. You, too, can live your life under the gaze of the Father who loves us. Under the influence of the transformative love of the Trinity, your heart can belong even now to the Father's House.

Reflection Questions

CHAPTER ONE

The Holy Trinity

1. How did I understand the purpose of my life before reading the chapter? Had I ever heard or thought about the connection between the question of my life's purpose and the mystery of the Holy Trinity?

2. How do I understand the purpose of life now after reading the chapter? Does the invitation to enter the Holy Trinity attract me? Why or why not?

3. How often do I think of the Holy Trinity throughout my day? How can I integrate meditation on the Trinity more into my daily life and prayers?

4. Which symbols in Rublev's icon of the Trinity were most illuminating?

5. How might I respond differently in the future to the claim that the Trinity is "just a mystery"?

CHAPTER TWO

To Be Jesus Christ

1. How did I understand my identity before reading this chapter? Did I ever previously connect the topic of identity with my Baptism?

2. How do I now understand my identity after reading this chapter? Does the invitation to union and identification with Jesus Christ appeal to me? Why or why not?

3. Upon hearing *you are Jesus*, what was my initial reaction: Wonder? Concern? Something else? Did any of the hesitations listed in this chapter resonate with me? Why or why not? How can I bring this reaction into my prayer life?

4. Do I think of my life as being one with the life of Jesus Christ? For example, do I ever think of my love for God as Jesus Christ's love for God burning in my own heart? Do I ever think of my sufferings as his sufferings? What might I do to remember such things in daily life? How might I pray with them to grow in union with Jesus?

5. What were the most difficult or challenging points in the chapter for me personally? What were the most enlightening or encouraging?

CHAPTER THREE
The Spirit of Love

1. What was my answer to the love question before reading this chapter? Did I ever connect the love question in my own heart with the Spirit of Love poured into our hearts at Baptism?

2. What is my answer to the love question now after reading the chapter? Does faith in the Spirit of Love make a difference in how I answer the question? Why or why not?

3. How have I experienced the Spirit of Love at work in my own heart and life? When have I been drawn to faith in Jesus Christ? In what ways?

4. Do I think of myself as a friend of God? Why or why not? If not, then how do I think of my relationship with God? How might that change after reading this chapter?

5. Have I experienced the Spirit of Love and *communio* in the Church? In what ways? Have I experienced disappointment and hurt in the Church? How have I reacted? After reading this chapter, has the way I see the Church changed? How so?

CHAPTER FOUR
The Pathos of the Heart

1. Have I ever thought of the following of Jesus Christ on the way of friendship as a path to the healing of my heart? Does doing so change how I understand Christianity? How so?

2. How did I think of the human heart before reading the chapter? How do I think of it after reading the chapter?

3. Does the description of the pathos of the heart in this chapter resonate with my own experience? In what ways?

4. Do I ever think that my sins or disordered thoughts define me? Why or why not? Does the distinction between the deep heart and the area around the heart, as well as the distinction between voluntary and involuntary *logismoi*, change how I understand myself? How so?

5. How does learning about the pathos of the heart change how I understand other people in the Church? How might it change my response to them?

CHAPTER FIVE
The Practicals of the Way

1. Have I experienced for myself how consistent practice of the Catholic faith can make a difference for the better in my life? Has it made a difference for the better in the lives of people whom I know? In what ways?

2. Have I ever thought of the following of Christ as a process of recovery for the eyes of my heart so that I might know the love of God more and more? In what ways must I change to keep the eyes of my heart more fixed on Jesus?

3. How did the discussion of the pathos of the heart in the previous chapter illuminate my interpretation of the law of love in this chapter? In which way do I find it most difficult to love God above all: with my heart, mind, soul, or strength?

4. Are there ways I can better practice the takeaways that go with the law of love? How might I better believe in God's love for me, watch at all times and pray, or do good to all?

5. What difference would it make to my understanding of morality if I thought of all moral laws and teachings as a light for the heart rather than simply as imposed obligations?

CHAPTER SIX

The Beatitudes

1. How did I understand the Beatitudes before reading this chapter? How do I understand them now after reading it?

2. If the Beatitudes depict the countenance of Christ and portray his charity, what should they mean to a disciple of Jesus Christ? If the Beatitudes are a summary of steps or a formation program for becoming another Christ in the world, what place do they have in discipleship? What place do they presently have in my own personal walk with the Lord?

3. Which Beatitude appeals the most to my own heart at present? Which one do I find most challenging to practice at present?

4. Which explanation of the Beatitudes was the most surprising? Which spoke to me the most? Which example or lesson from the lives of the saints was most inspirational? Why?

5. How might I better ponder the Beatitudes, pray for the grace of the Beatitudes, and practice the Beatitudes in my daily walk with Jesus Christ?

CHAPTER SEVEN
The Father's House

1. How has my experience of human fatherhood affected my understanding of the eternal Father?

2. Has this chapter changed my understanding of what fatherhood is? Has it changed my understanding of the heavenly Father? How so?

3. Do the five roles of fathers in ancient Israel speak to the role of fathers today? In what ways?

4. Has the mystery of the Father's House in heaven touched my own life on earth? In what ways?

5. What were the most illuminating points in the chapter? What were the most challenging?

CHAPTER EIGHT
The Mystery of Filial Adoption

1. How does hearing about the mystery of my own filial adoption in Baptism affect my relationship with God? How does it affect my understanding of my prayer life?

2. Does the call to contemplative prayer draw me? Have I already experienced the Presence of God in my life in some ways? In what ways?

3. Is the real presence of Christ in the Eucharist easy or hard to believe in? Why?

4. Have I ever thought of the Eucharist as something from the Father's House in the heavenly places actually present here on the earth? Have I ever thought of my prayer in the Mass, or Divine Liturgy, as a participation in Jesus' prayer and offering to the Father? What difference could it make in my life to think in this way?

5. Has the book as a whole changed my answers to the three questions? Has it changed how I plan to live? If so, how?

Prayer to the Holy Trinity

O MY GOD, Trinity whom I adore, help me to forget myself entirely that I may be established in You as still and as peaceful as if my soul were already in eternity. May nothing trouble my peace or make me leave You, O my Unchanging One, but may each minute carry me further into the depths of Your Mystery. Give peace to my soul; make it Your heaven, Your beloved dwelling and Your resting place. May I never leave You there alone but be wholly present, my faith wholly vigilant, wholly adoring, and wholly surrendered to Your creative Action.

O my beloved Christ, crucified by love, I wish to be a bride for Your Heart; I wish to cover You with glory; I wish to love You . . . even unto death! But I feel my weakness, and I ask You to "clothe me with Yourself," to identify my soul with all the movements of Your Soul, to overwhelm me, to possess me, to substitute Yourself for me that my life may be but a radiance of Your Life. Come into me as Adorer, as Restorer, as Savior. O Eternal Word, Word of my God, I want to spend my life in listening to You, to become wholly teachable that I may learn all from You. Then, through all nights, all voids, all help-lessness, I want to gaze on You always and remain in Your great light. O my beloved Star, so fascinate me that I may not withdraw from Your radiance.

O consuming Fire, Spirit of Love, "come upon me," and create in my soul a kind of incarnation of the Word: that I may be another humanity for Him in which He can renew His whole Mystery. And You, O Father, bend lovingly over Your poor little creature; "cover her with Your shadow," seeing in her only the "Beloved in whom You are well pleased."

O my Three, my All, my Beatitude, infinite Solitude, Immensity in which I lose myself, I surrender myself to You as Your prey. Bury Yourself in me that I may bury myself in You until I depart to contemplate in Your light the abyss of Your greatness.

SAINT ELIZABETH OF THE TRINITY
+ *November 21, 1904*[78]

---

78. *The Complete Works of Elizabeth of the Trinity*, vol. 1, 183–184.

Pauline
BOOKS & MEDIA

A mission of the Daughters of St. Paul

As apostles of Jesus Christ,
evangelizing today's world:

We are CALLED to holiness
by God's living Word and Eucharist.

We COMMUNICATE the Gospel message
through our lives and through all
available forms of media.

We SERVE the Church
by responding to the hopes and needs
of all people with the Word of God,
in the spirit of St. Paul.

For more information visit us at:
www.pauline.org